Praise for

Sindiwe Magona's
To My Children's Children

"Magona's memoir is a delightful, poignant, feisty and uplifting story that chronicles, in a refreshing and authentic voice, what it means to attain womanhood in a society where patriarchy and apartheid often conspired to degrade and enslave women economically, domestically, politically, traditionally and sexually."

— *Washington Post Book World*

"Sindiwe Magona writes with vibrance and intimacy. [She] offers the reader deep insight into life under apartheid."

— *Everywoman (London)*

"Reading Sindiwe Magona's celebratory autobiography is like holding a handful of bright African beads; each tale and her telling of it is part of the treasure; you are affected and altered… It is a bold, spirited, funny book… one of the best…"

— *Argus*

"Her tale is about a special past; about the joys, pains, love and enmity which befalls blacks in varying degrees, and at the various levels of human conduct… I read and relished Magona's vividly written account about her sheltered and protected childhood; about the pain and trauma of dislocation, schooling, death and womanhood… the crystal-clear voice of a dignified, proud yet humble, and graceful woman. A book to read."

—*The Weekly Mail (South Africa)*

"It is extremely difficult for a black writer to maintain a sense of humor and optimism when writing about life in South Africa… Sindiwe Magona's sensitive and lively account of her childhood and early adulthood, however, is refreshingly free from the characteristic self-pitying sentimentality which sometimes weaken the powerful social criticism this kind of writing intends to make… such powerful self-revelation finally confirms that this emergent writer has set new standards for protest writing."

—*South*

"Not only is Magona's story worth telling, but her use of language is so masterly that it becomes a delight in itself… [A] highly readable book. Incidents are always recounted with humour and wit and her descriptions of people she meets is nothing short of inspired."

— *Literary Review*

"More than simply an account of her own life, Sindiwe Magona's *To My Children's Children* is a reflection of the struggle faced by all black South African women not only against Apartheid but also against their own culture and people… It's gripping and comprehensive, dragging the reader from sympathy to sorrow, laughter to anger... Sindiwe Magona could become the next cult name amongst black women writers — she certainly has some stories to tell."

—Laura Manison, University of Cardiff

"Autobiography at its finest, where the self-portrait also becomes a canvas of a suppressed people, writing in dignity... struggling for justice and a new nationhood."

—Morning Star

Praise for

Living, Loving and Lying Awake at Night

"Sindiwe Magona's *Living, Loving and Lying Awake at Night* rips away apartheid's shroud which hovers over lives, loves and losses of South African women with a ferocity that is both startling and enlightening... [It] is a riveting look at the triumph of will and spirit in the face of apartheid's dehumanization. Magona has given us endearing characters and probing stories that are as authoritative as they are unforgettable.

— Quarterly Black Review of Books

"Magona is a storyteller centered in her power, convinced of the universal relevance of what she sees. The effect is felt like the strong South African sun, each story's momentum like the pounding of a drum."

—Booklist

"Her book is of excruciating beauty and yet covered by a mantle of hope and love... From the very first lines of this book you know you are in the hands of a powerful wordmaker..."

— Morning Star (London)

"*Living, Loving and Lying Awake at Night* confirms her ability to speak on behalf of African women with an acuity that is frequently very funny, often achingly sad... Magona's rendition of the tragicomedy of the lives of disadvantaged South African women is so sharply done one can almost believe it's all fiction."

— Cosmopolitan (London)

"The outstanding feature of *Living, Loving and Lying Awake at Night* is the style: a soliloquy which rarely becomes a dialogue."

—World Literature Today

"A superb collection of short stories bringing a full range of South African women's experiences brilliantly to light... this collection is at once tragic, triumphant, humorous and sharp, but above all, forcefully empowering."

—Feminist Bookstore News

To My Children's Children

SINDIWE MAGONA

INTERLINK BOOKS

An imprint of Interlink Publishing Group, Inc.

NEW YORK

This edition first published 1998 by

INTERLINK BOOKS
An imprint of Interlink Publishing Group, Inc.
99 Seventh Avenue · Brooklyn, New York 11215 and
46 Crosby Street · Northampton, Massachusetts 01060

Originally published in South Africa by
David Philip Publishers (Pty) Ltd.

Library of Congress Cataloging-in-Publication Data

Magona, Sindiwe
    To my children's children / Sindiwe Magona.
        p.   cm.
    ISBN 1-56656-163-9 — ISBN 1-56656-294-5 (pbk.)
    1. Magona, Sindiwe—Biography.   2. Women authors, South
African—20th century—Biography. 3. Family—South Africa.
I. Title.
PR9369.3.M335Z47   1998
823—dc20
[B]   94-4358
                                                            CIP

Printed and bound in Canada
10 9 8 7 6 5 4 3 2 1

To order or request our complete catalog,
please call us at **1-800-238-LINK** or write to:
Interlink Publishing
46 Crosby Street, Northampton, MA 01060
e-mail: interpg@aol.com · website: www.interlinkbooks.com

Contents

For Thembeka, Thokozile
and Sandile,
my children
who brought me up

Preface

FROM A XHOSA GRANDMOTHER

When I am old, wrinkled, and gray, what shall I tell you, my great-granddaughter? What memories will stay with me of days of yester-year? Of my childhood, what shall I remember? What of my young womanhood, my wifehood, and motherhood? Work has been a big part of my life. Of that, what memories will linger, what nightmares haunt me forever? How will you know who you are if I do not or cannot tell you the story of your past?

Early days

Child of the Child of My Child
    As ours is an oral tradition I would like you to hear from my own lips what it was like living in the 1940s onwards. What it was like in the times of your great-grandmother, me.

However, my people no longer live long lives. Generations no longer set eyes on one another. Therefore, I fear I may not live long enough to do my duty to you, to let you know who you are and whence you are. So, I will keep, for you, my words in this manner:

I was born in the Union of South Africa before Great Britain handed over our land to the Afrikaner; before the pounds, shillings, and pennies we grew up with gave way to rands and cents. Then, we were called Natives by polite white people, and kaffirs by the not polite ones, basking in the impunity they enjoyed before the law.

THE LAW! The greatest hardship we labored under was not that we had no protection from the law. No! That was the lesser evil. The worst was that we were burdened with protection by the master

1

race via an unwieldy plethora of laws, by-laws, rules and regulations passed by a parliament with whose existence we had had naught to do and whose raison d'être appeared to be our exclusive "protection."

Heavy, indeed, was the yoke that black people bore, thus protected by the white man who had set himself up as their god.

As far back as I can remember, there has always been a place to which I belonged with a certainty that nothing has been able to take from me. When I say place, that means less a geographical locality and more a group of people with whom I am connected and to whom I belong. This is a given, a constant in my life.

The second of eight children, of whom seven survived to adulthood, I am the eldest of five daughters.

My recollections of myself, as a little girl of three or four, revolve around my great-grandmother, Nophuthukezi, my two grandmothers, my mother, and my maternal grandfather. My paternal grandfather is there, but in a rather shadowy way. I do not see him as often as I see the others.

My father, in these early mind-pictures, is even more of a shadow than his father. I remember him, even then, as a stern, unsmiling man with a low but resonant voice and a deliberate gait — as serious as a funeral. Even the droop on the left side of his upper lip failed to alleviate the severity of father's appearance. Overripe-berry-brown skin stretched over the face, way back, past where the hairline should have been. This, in my mind, set him apart as old and wise. (Father had married at twenty-eight, already bald.) Legend had it that baldness heralded wealth. I grew up therefore convinced of father's wisdom and our impending abundance.

Although he was not tall, he seemed so to me; tall, sturdy, and strong.

This sense of his being powerful would never leave me. Even when I saw him, a man of sixty-three, lying in a hospital bed, riddled with cancer; I looked at him, knowing he was going, but I still saw that enormous strength.

He worked in Cape Town and came to see us once in a long while. That was not unusual. Then, as now, villages in South Africa were peopled by women, children, and those men who were either old or disabled. Able-bodied African men were in the cities where the mines and the farms and industrial complexes swallow them. The law forbade them to bring their families.

Father's visits were brief, too brief for me to get to know him. Not that I recall any such desire, on my part. We didn't even call him "*tata*" (father). He was called "*Bhuti waseKapa*" (older brother from Cape Town) by mother's siblings, too young to use the customary "*Sibali*" (brother-in-law). We, his three children, addressed him similarly, imitating them.

However, to his children he has towered large from age five to six until now, although he has been gone these fifteen years or more, and most of us who were children together already have grandchildren.

As I have mentioned, I lived with my maternal grandparents. We lived in Gungululu, where I was born. Gungululu is a village about eleven miles from Umtata, a little town in the then Cape Province of the Union of South Africa. Born just before the end of the Second World War, when South Africa was still a British colony, at birth I was, therefore, a South African citizen.

It is customary among amaXhosa, my people, for the eldest child or the elder children of a marriage to live with one or the other set of grandparents. My eldest brother, Jongilizwe, our younger sister (at that time), Siziwe, and I were not the only grandchildren in this homestead. Mandla, my mother's eldest brother's first-born, lived with us. There were several other cousins, once, twice, and several times removed, who, in the nature of kinship among us, shared our home, albeit with less permanency.

The intricate ways in which relationships are drawn among us make it almost impossible for an individual to be destitute in the sense of having connections with no living soul. One could, conceivably, be minus parent, or issue; have neither spouse nor sibling; but to be alone, with no relative, no one to care for or to lean on, is virtually unheard of except in the very rare case of an individual of such an unbearable and odious disposition that no one can stand him or her or be moved to pity at the plight of such a one. Someone met today, completely unknown before, is a relative one cannot even think of marrying if that person is of the same clan name.

In such a people-world, filled with a real, immediate, and tangible sense of belongingness, did I spend the earliest years of my life. I was not only wanted, I was loved. I was cherished.

The adults in my world, no doubt, had their cares and their sorrows. But childhood, by its very nature, is a magic-filled world, egocentric, wonderfully carefree, and innocent. Mine was all these things and more.

There was mother, who was sometimes with us but lived at her husband's, my father's, home. In my mind the distinction is of little importance. The two homesteads were both home to me. I was equally welcome at both. Fed and washed and combed at both, I accepted, without question, that both were my home. People in the one were as good to me as those in the other. I called MaXolo, my paternal grandmother, "Makhulu." That is also what I called MaMkwayi, my mother's mother. Mama called both women "Mama," for that is the custom among amaXhosa; when one marries into a family, one is an addition to that family in its blessed extended completeness.

Though the days had their own treasures, it was the nights that brought the whole family together in a magic circle as the prelude to refreshing, restoring, restful sleep: night was heralded by the live-stock — chickens, goats, pigs, sheep, cattle, and horses, all being shepherded into their various enclosures and padlocked. The responsibility for each of these groups of animals was allocated to specific individuals and mostly fell on the younger boys and girls; the older assuming more the roles of overseers, and grandfather, with grand-mother as his right hand, monitoring everything.

As soon as a child can walk and talk, that child is given tasks to perform, even if those tasks are in the form of "helping" someone else. Sweeping, carrying water from the river, feeding the chickens and collecting eggs, fetching firewood, stoking the fire, grinding or stamping corn: relative to a little girl's age, these were some of the tasks I was given. Boys usually milk the cows, goats, and sheep; and also herd the livestock.

By dusk all the animals are in, the evening meal is cooking, the little ones are having a hard time keeping awake. Babies are put to sleep having been fed.

By age three I had a baby sister and was, by definition, no longer a baby and thus qualified to sit around the fire with the other children, waiting for the evening meal and evening prayers thereafter.

4

The grown-ups busied themselves with evening chores; among the last, putting the grass mats on which we slept (perhaps less than one per cent of the village had beds) in place. Some, at this time, would be preparing what would be breakfast the following day.

Always, however, there was at least one adult, usually grandmama, sitting with us around the fire. To keep us children awake, she would tell us *iintsomi*, the fairy tales of amaXhosa.

There were tales about ogres and giants, about animals of the forests, great beasts, and about little hopping creatures of the veld. There were tales about animals of the river, huge scale-covered reptiles that could swallow people and animals whole, crushing them to death as they did so. And later on, when hungry, bring them up and chew them as cud.

There were happy tales also: princes and princesses, kings and queens, and chiefs and chieftainesses; stories that we listened to and believed. Stories that were told with such vivid detail and in such modulation of voice that we children saw them in our minds and lived them in our feelings; crying when a little orphaned girl, on her way to her uncle or her grandparents who would look after her (this would-be guardian angel always lived far, far away) fell into the hands of an ogre disguised as a kindly little old lady, with designs to have her for his dinner. We roared with laughter — the kind of laughter that leaves you feeling weak in your belly, tears streaming down your face; honest no-nonsense and no-decorum laughter — whenever cruel giants and cannibals came to grief, usually by inadvertently falling prey to the very traps intended for their victims.

Oh, no doubt, we were blood-thirsty little people ourselves, but we felt self-righteous about it as long as it was the bad, terrible, cruel, ugly ogre, or some such, who thus met his demise.

Some of these stories told us of the origin of man, others were about natural phenomena, and others still were designed to teach us, the unwary audience, some aspect of morality. Looking back now, I can see clearly how *iintsomi* are an essential and integral part of the socialization of the child among amaXhosa. The lazy youngster who would not bother to learn from his or her elders was punished: usually he or she ended up without a spouse because no one would marry such a sluggard. Always, good behavior was rewarded and bad punished.

Central to the stories in which people featured, was the bond of love with the concomitants: duty, obedience, responsibility, honor, and orderliness; always orderliness. Like the seasons of the year, life was depicted full of cause and effect, predictability and order; connectedness and oneness.

Often repeated, by their variety and abundance *iintsomi* could never become boring, and I have heard the same sounding fresh each time when told by a different person, or even by the same person with difference of nuance, with embellishment, with different modulation of voice, and different choice of words.

Both men and women tell folktales to children. These stories are handed down, by word of mouth, from generation to generation. In my own family, the outstanding storytellers of my childhood were my maternal grandmother, a paternal uncle, Masondo, and a cousin, Sondlo. When either of these two men came to visit, we would listen to their tales well into the night, willingly warding off sleep. They were masters of the art.

Sometimes other games were introduced of an evening. Sparks on the three-legged cast-iron pot, sparks produced by scratching the pot on the fire with one of the logs burning underneath, become *"abayeni,"* the team of negotiators for a daughter's hand in marriage.

An uncle or aunt will say, "Let us see how many *abayeni* will come to ask for so and so one day" (naming one of the little girls present).

So saying, they will take one of the little sticks of wood burning under the pot and scratch the side of the pot with one bold stroke. Immediately, sparks will become visible where the pot has been scratched. Everyone, especially the one-distant-day bride to be, is now spellbound. The counting begins:

"One, two, three, four, five . . ."

"Goodness!" someone else will butt in. "Where will we put such a big party?"

Another will ask, "How will we feed so many people?"

"Girl, it looks like you will marry into a well-to-do family; otherwise how could they send so many people?"

This little game ends with much leg-pulling and laughter and no little sense of importance in the future bride.

When we were older and had come to live with her, mother often made us first do some special chore if we wanted her to tell us tales. This somewhat detracted from our enjoyment of them, no doubt the desired outcome.

By that time we had moved away from the village and, consequently, all the chores of a homemaker fell solely on her shoulders. Nightfall probably found her hunting-dog tired: the last thing on her mind, tales and games.

It was in such a warm human environment that I spent the first five years of my life. I had much attention, much discipline, much loving, much caring, much play, much work; in short, total immersion into a group where my own place in it was clearly defined. This arrangement I accepted as a given, for there was nothing peculiar or particularly noteworthy about it; it was how things were in the late forties among amaXhosa in the Transkeian region of the Cape Province of the Union of South Africa. I was happy. I was loved. And my world seemed safe and secure.

To us children, the whole village was a mystery-filled expanse; awaiting, during the day, our discovery: things to seek, things to do, things to make, things to eat, things forbidden, some even dangerous, according to our own overworked imagination.

All these were there for us to find and enjoy or to fear and be tantalized by. I remember rag dolls that both Makhulu MaMkwayi and Makhulu MaXolo made for me. They were fun. Tremendous fun. And I loved them, played with them and reveled in dressing them myself. But, is there any comparison between playing house and the heady exhilaration of skipping naked in the light summer showers singing, in unison, with complete abandon:

"Nqaphela, ndikhule!	"Be stunted, that I grow!
"Nqaphela, ndikhule!	"Be stunted, that I grow!
"Nqaphela, ndikhule!"	"Be stunted, that I grow!"

The utter selfishness, bordering on malice, contained in such a wish, was lost on each child, happy in the group activity.

Rhymes such as this one, as also the tales, have been handed down, by word of mouth, from generation to generation. Whatever evil intent, if any, might have been contained in them originally, has been lost. However, my playmates must have had louder voices, for whoever we were addressing with our unconscious prayers must have heard only their voices and not mine. I am under five foot, in high heels.

And then there was the river. Dividing the village into lower and upper Gungululu. A phenomenon. The river also divided the children into those who were big enough to cross it and the little ones, those who couldn't. The latter group was made up of those who couldn't because given their age they were physically incapable of the task, and the cowards whose hearts pounded like drums at the very thought of crossing it. All were lumped together as the little ones who can't go across. Those who were little in years had hope. The others were sub-ject to daily teasing until they overcame their fear and crossed over.

How we all loved the river!

Wading in the shallow water and trying to catch tadpoles was a favored pastime. These tiny creatures are small, slippery, and swift in slicing through little fingers clumsily closing in a vain attempt to capture them. Often I would be certain I had one in my hands but, opening them, would be astonished to find them empty. There was no reason for hunting tadpoles except the challenge that catching them presented. We would wager bets as to who would have the biggest catch or be the first to make one.

This activity was one our parents did not encourage. We could drown. We could slip on the mossy stones on the river-bed and hurt ourselves. We could catch a cold from getting wet. We could be "called into" (*sibizelwe*) the river by Mamlambo, the River Woman whose dangerous beauty grew people into the depth of her magnetic eyes, sucked them into the world deep under the river, where she made her home.

For the most part, these were objections that we chose to ignore: death doesn't frighten the very young. To them, it is as distant as a lifetime; something vaguely associated with gray hair and wrinkles. How else would we have touched, smelled, tasted of so much of the richness of the river? The yellowish-green blanket of the frogs? The tasteless dirty-white foamy sweat of water that has come gurgling, spiraling and spilling over boulders to rest at one of the many elbows of the river, catching its breath and breaking into sweat, before wending

8

its way and making room for wearier water? The unsightly frogs and their graceful sometimes jerky movements? What of those dark green reeds whose yellowish-white tender stalks, just above the roots, are such sweet delicacies?

In summer, when days stretched endlessly, this was our favorite playground. We swam in the river, bathed in the river, fetched water from it, and washed clothes in it. But most important of all, we played in it. I still do not know how the water remains clean in the river when each village makes so much use of it, and in so many different ways.

Just as important, was the veld. The veld offered space to be in, to run, to play, to scour, and to roam. There, to run and run and run; with not a fence for miles, as far as the eye could see. To run and feel the grass massage your feet and, on a wet day, betray you into an unceremonious skid.

Boys hunted birds and small animals such as fieldmice, moles, and rabbits. We girls would gather berries and dig for wild roots. And all this fare was for us children to roast or cook and eat. Of course, the berries and the roots were ready to pop into watering mouth as soon as possible.

Do not, for a minute, suppose that having thus fed ourselves we would not partake of the regular family meals. We have a saying amongst our people, *"ukutya komny'umz'akuhluthisi"* (another home's fare never satisfies). The implication is that one will eat anywhere but can never be truly satisfied until one has had something to eat at home.

This same veld offered grazing for our livestock and yielded *umfino*, wild spinach, to our mothers, in rich variety. There too, the witchdoctor dug for roots and harvested healing herbs. And, those of us with liver enough to do so, hid until kingdom come in the deep red-earth dongas.

There, we played "hide and seek" knowing nothing of the dongas' ominous meaning, the impoverishment of the land as the topsoil washed away. Only the evil things said to make their home in the dongas — *ootikoloshe*, the little people, and *izithunzela*, the zombies — sometimes gave us cause for concern.

I do not remember ever being desperately hungry as a child. No.

There was always more than enough to eat. New mealies cooked on the cob, dry mealies cooked with beans, mealies roasted, mealies stamped and broken into bits, mealies crushed and ground to powder; pumpkin as vegetable, pumpkin mixed with mealie-meal, other squash, eggs, fruit, sour milk, milk fresh foamy warm, straight from the udder; garden vegetable, wild vegetable, *amazimba*, and a host of other delectable eatables. Such variety; such ready availability!

Like comets, strange people from another world occasionally ruffled our even-keeled existence.

"Nab'abelungu! Nab'abelungu!" (Here are white people!) The shout is followed by a flurry of activity as each one of us abruptly abandons whatever activity we have been engrossed in only a minute before, reaching for our wares, grabbing-running towards the tarred road that snakes through the village of mud-walled grass-thatched huts. Panting, we reach the road as the cars that excited the cry cruise slowly past or, as if to pass but reluctant to miss this live part of the picturesque that the tour guide books had promised, come to an idling stop.

Fascinated, I look. Whirling thoughts arrested to detail. Yes, it is true! *Abelungu* do have eyes colored like those of cats. Jongi, who had seen such people at the shop, had tried often to explain what they looked like. In meeting them for myself, I decided he had left a lot unexplained. What was wrong with their feet? Without a single exception, they all wore shoes.

Even mother's explanation later would not satisfy me: "Their bodies are like those of babies, so their feet would be hurt by the ground if they didn't wear shoes." All sensible; except, the babies I knew were busy crawling and running around on the same grass, with not a stitch on.

The passengers stare. We stare right back. Both curious. We awed, admiring, scared, and confused. And, in an unformed way, knowing that we were a motif in something bigger, powerful, and all pervasive: understanding and not knowing. Not knowing but understanding. We — Them.

Proudly presenting our goods, boldly we approach the cars. I must have been four years old then because father came and took us to Cape Town when I was five years old and my eldest brother seven.

They said something, we replied. I can't recall the words they said for I never understood them even as they were being said. The only thing that convinced me they were words, or, rather, that words had been said, were the sounds I heard and the lips, I could barely distinguish, that moved. But then, I also believed thunder was God speaking!

That whatever they said was nothing I understood simplified our transaction for me. By taking away the need for comprehension, I was left unhindered and unhampered by having to strive for coherence. Since what they said was incomprehensible to me, it followed that if, in reply, I said some incomprehensible nonsense, they would understand it perfectly, that being their way of talking.

The logic of a child facilitated what now, as an adult, I find excruciatingly difficult; communication:

"Shwe-shwehn-shwehn shwehn," we heard them say.

"Shwen, shwe-shwen," we replied.

We addressed them in the gibberish they spoke. Hands almost met. We had the money. They had the goods. Some gave us pennies, ha'pennies, and a few, even, "the money with birds" — farthings, worthless. However, I remember there were some who gave us shiny silver coins. Tickeys? Sixpences? More? Who knows? Maybe there were even some florins and half crowns there. We never complained, whatever we got. A big part of our trade was the sense of adventure, the excitement, this activity afforded us.

The road was not very far from our homes; but still, it was out of bounds. Although a car was a rare sighting in our part of the country, its potential danger was well advertised, if not exaggerated.

Our customers left with waves and hoots. We remained completely oblivious to our contribution to their general well-being whilst on vacation. What they did with the crudely molded resin stuck on tiny twigs, is anybody's guess. No one could have mistaken that for a lollipop. Well, on the other hand, some people cast coins into wishing-wells. When we have a feast we spill beer on the ground before drinking that the ancestors may partake thereof, be pleased with us for remembering them, and, thus pacified, intercede on our behalf, mediating for our welfare. We ate resin. I still do. How were we to know that they did not? Food is food. Then, I did not know that the French eat frogs but I never will.

11

Another evening, we are sitting around the fire in the Big Hut. All the huts have names; not dining-room or bedroom kind of names: Ethekwini (in Durban), uXande (the pantry), eNdlin'enkulu (in the Big Hut), are the only names I remember, although I am convinced there were more than three huts in my maternal grandparents' home.

The Big Hut is the family room where most of the living is done. We cook here. We eat here. It is where people sit and talk or just sit and be. In the center of the hut a black cast-iron three-legged pot stands. Underneath, a fire burns steadily with a lazy flame. Stamped mealies, with beans, the staple food of amaXhosa, nutritious because of the beans, is cooking. This is supper.

We children wait, hardly able to keep our upper and lower lids from kissing, and kissing becoming forever sewn in sleep till the next day.

Grandmother, to prevent our falling asleep, begins what is the evening ritual: *"Kwathi ke kaloku ngantsomi . . .,"* the Xhosa "Once Upon a Time."

Many are the tales I have listened to as a child. Another night a visitor, perhaps an uncle, will undertake to amuse the children:

"Qashi, qashi!" he begins and we are all agog, each trying to be the first to guess the riddle he is about to pose.

"Qashi, qashi. Ndinahashe lam Aliphali lingenamsila!"

"Guess, guess, I have
This horse of mine
   That will not gallop
   Without a tail!"

"Qashi, Qashi,
Ndinamadoda am alishumi
Aphuma esiya kuzingela
Ehlathini elikhulu elimnyama
Oshumi ayazingela
Kodw'akufumana
Mabini qha atyayo!"
and
"Qashi, qashi
Ndinabantu bam babini
Bemi phantsi kwamawa

"Guess, guess,
I have these ten men
Who set out to hunt
In a big, black forest.
   All ten hunt but
   When the game is caught
Only two do feast!"

Guess, guess, I have these
Two people standing
Under twin cliffs.

TO MY CHILDREN'S CHILDREN

Baphala ngumbane	Like lightning so swift
Ngephanyazo bawela	A flash is all it takes
Imilambo bee gxada	For them to leap across
Kwiindul' ezikude!"	Rivers to yonder hills!"

And more, and more, until another game is decided on or tyrannical sleep summons.

These riddles, as most of our games, relied heavily on the cost-free: observation, memory, our own bodies, bits and pieces from the environment, discarded articles from our daily living — all these were knitted with the rich thread of magic and imagination, providing children and adults alike with endless diversion.

The "solution" to the above riddles bears witness to their source, our life: (not in order) the eyes; a needle pulling thread; fingers, the head and lice!

The gleefulness of the days was punctuated by the peculiarity of Sunday. Not only were chores not done but everything else went upside down: even the clothes we wore were stiff and joyless. I would wear my Sunday dress, the newest I had, reserved for going to church.

Sundays were subdued sorry dull days on which the possibility of any fun was effectively erased. It was a day to get up early, very early; get washed, very thoroughly, under adult supervision with none of the hit or miss affair of a regular day when, if the intricacies of wetting hands, soaping hands, rubbing soaped and hopefully, still soapy hands on part of body targeted for cleaning, then scooping water from the basin, and, with joined hands carrying it to same areas as was soaped . . . rubbing, scooping, rinsing . . . might or might not have the desired result.

The Day of the Lord was a careful day; correct and thoroughly ill at ease. In the orderly procession to church, we children were made to walk in front of the grown-ups. In church, we were made to sit quietly; stand when the congregation did so and sit when it sat. "Do not talk. Do not look around. Do not cough. Do not go out. Do not . . . do not . . . do not." Oh, there were so many prohibitions attending Sunday, it is a day on which, even now, I find I cannot relax.

The reluctant memories of Sundays that I carry are as uninspiring as the singing I suffered through at church. They are a little frightened, maybe in recollection of the fire, brimstone, and gnashing of teeth that was promised in almost every sermon that I had the misfortune to pay attention to: hope of salvation eluded me particularly on Sundays. The conditions of attaining it appeared too high for anyone, but definitely out of my sinful reach.

Had I not envied another a toy or a dress? Had I not lied perhaps to save myself more immediate punishment? Had I not stolen — sugar, milk, or some such? Had I not been lazy or reluctant in doing my chores?

If I learnt anything in church, it was how certainly I was doomed to burn in hell. It seemed very unfair that "we sin by deed, word, or thought." And I was told these ways of transgression carried equal weight. I was confounded. Even when I refrained from doing wrong I had already sinned. Why is it impossible for the mind to stop itself from thinking sinful thoughts before it starts thinking them? I knew, and my daily wickedness confirmed this, I was beyond redemption.

2

Then, my child, your great-great-grandmother, my mother, took ill and had to go and join father in Cape Town where she would be near good doctors and good hospitals; a not difficult thing to decide since there was neither doctor nor hospital in Gungululu.

Not long after mother's departure, Grandmother MaMkwayi died. This necessitated our going to live with our parents in Cape Town.

We were very lucky Makhulu MaMkwayi died when she did. A year later, 1948, the Boers came into power. Among the first laws the new government passed were those severely restricting the movement of Africans. So if our grandmother had died two years later it would have been extremely difficult, if not impossible, for us to join our parents.

This positive outcome, like so many of the factors that have determined my life, did not ensue from any meticulous planning. I am the result of a series of losses, lacks, and lapses.

Following MaMkwayi's passing away, we could have gone to live

14

with our other grandmother, MaXolo. However, that lady had been abandoned early in their marriage by her husband, my paternal grandfather. He had left her expecting their first, and, as it turned out, only child, my father, and gone to Johannesburg's mines. When he returned, father was ten years old and she had long been released by her in-laws. She had remarried and had another family. So although we were her grandchildren, since she was no longer married to our grandfather I guess decorum dictated we should not go and stay with her.

Like most of my playmates, I was growing up fatherless. I had seen father two or three times, I think, before this. That was a year of many changes for me. The year was 1947.

This news that we were going to Cape Town caused much excitement, not only to the two of us but also to our playmates, as would be hard to imagine.

We, who had not been on a car or a bus; who had not been even to Tsolo, the one-dirt-road town which, from the village, lay in the opposite direction to Umtata but a little further away, or so I understood — we were going, BY TRAIN, to Cape Town.

Of course, we had no idea of the distance between Umtata and Cape Town but we were excited by the very thought of traveling, of going, of going away, far away, somewhere, anywhere. No jetsetter ever felt more important, nor astronaut more adventurous.

For weeks preceding this unexpected event we, in our new and elevated status, in the eyes of our mates, received a lot of advice on how to wind up our affairs in the village. My brother gave his clay cattle to a very trusted friend to keep for him until his return. For some reason I have not been able to fathom to this day, the same friend was not trusted with Jongi's cars. But then, although I didn't understand why he gave one of the smoothed stones to grandfather and buried the other amidst the roots of one of the gum trees behind the homestead, I wasn't about to reveal the enormity of my ignorance by asking him for an explanation of his actions.

When a girl is all of five years and has a brother — taller, two years older, a brother who has attained rites of passage to the foreboding building called school, a brother who can read, write, knows English words, does sums, can run and win races, cross the river to the next village, go with the older kids to the village shop where there are the white people, with hair like the silken threads that form a golden slip around the kernels of corn on cob, protecting it from the harsher green skirt covering it — that girl has to take great care always to prove worthy of having, as occasional companion, a brother such as that. My great fortune was not lost on me.

I had no cattle. But I did have dolls, rag dolls that my grandmothers had made for me. Not slow in learning the ways of the worldly, I buried one of my dolls and gave one to grandmother MaXolo. Even at that age I must have known one did not saddle men with such mundane things as children! The other two, I entrusted to my best friend, Noni, who, nearly forty years since, I have not seen again.

Something in me must have not felt quite right about burying one of my babies. Under cover of night, my last night in Gungululu, I went and unburied my doll. However, my sense of shame at this weakness made me leave the doll behind one of the rondavels, promising to bring it inside later that night when my brother would be asleep.

There was never any question of taking any of the rag dolls to Cape Town with me. Even I knew it would have been ridiculous to take a rag doll to the big big faraway town where there were many many people who were white just like the white people of the shop; where there were tens and tens and tens of motor cars, maybe hundreds, on the tar-covered roads; where everyone went by bus or train even if they were going half the distance we traveled on foot going to church every Sunday. Where there were no mud huts but brick and cement and stone houses, their windows made of glass not wood. And the roofs were made not of dull-colored grass but shiny metal; zinc roofs. Where everyone ate meat every day and did not have to wait until there was a feast or one of the cattle was dying or dead before they could have meat. What fool would take a rag doll to such a place?

Talking about Cape Town, we made ourselves quite knowledgeable on the subject. Later, years later, no geography teacher would ever kindle in me fiery enthusiasm even remotely approximating this level of curiousness, imaginativeness, and razor keenness about a place, its people, and its ways.

There were no tears at parting, for we did not fully understand the meaning of the event; we did not realize we might never again see most of those dear ones we were leaving behind: my maternal grandfather would die without my ever seeing him again. Father's father we would see once more because he would come to Cape Town, almost three decades later, to bury his son. Only MaXolo, of my beloved grandparents, would live not only to see my own children but to get to know them a little.

We had no way of knowing the tremendous financial sacrifice father was making in coming to take us to be near his place of employment; nor did we, because of our youth, realize that not every pregnant woman will hold an infant in her arms or suckle one.

The promise of Cape Town!

3

Thus did I, at age five, begin experiencing life in the nuclear family. Away from familiar faces, familiar customs, and the security of the known.

"Kubo-ooo-oo-oooooo-mvu! Kubooo-oo-ooo-omvu! (It is red! It is red!)

We had not been in our new home in Blaauvlei Location a week when we were awakened by this piercing, almost ullulating cry, breaking the stillness of the night as some unknown woman alerted others, unknown to her, of the presence of the police. The cry was taken on and passed on and on and on, by faceless other women to yet others, faceless and unknown.

As if this shattering of the inky night was not unsettling in itself, my usually sedate mother sprang up from her bed like someone who had had a terrible nightmare about a puffadder in her bed only to wake up and discover the object of her dream writhing beneath her. She hastily dressed, took a bag, stealthily opened the door, peered furtively into the staring blacker blackness, exited without closing the door, only pulling it to. Her movements, all this time, were those of a thief.

We children, by some instinctive self-preservation knowledge, knew better than to let anyone see we were awake, never mind ask questions.

Throughout this activity, father was grumbling and mumbling in a manner disapproving. Mother came back, threw the now-empty bag on top of the cupboard; hastily removed the wrap-around pinafore she had thrown over her flannel petticoat that doubled as nightie.

There was loud banging at the door accompanied by —

"Hey, *vula!* Open up! *Vula!* Police! *Vula!*"

Seconds later, father having put on pants and opened the door to the loud raps of police sticks on it, piercing torches searched our eyes; blankets were rudely pulled away; loud foreign voices demanded names and relations of those in the house. Eyes followed flashlights into cupboard, under bed, under table, into nooks, into crannies; sticks prodded floorboards, sticks prodded ceiling cardboard, sticks prodded newspaper-papered walls. Finally, grudgingly, the police left and we all went back to sleep.

Except for the thundering of my own heart, not a word had passed between us during the presence of the police. Not a word was spoken after they had left. Knowledge I would hide, for years even from myself, became mine that night: Father's eyes also could house fear.

I had just witnessed my first liquor raid. It was a Friday night.

Possession of liquor by an African was forbidden by law. To remedy that situation, the African locations sprouted shebeens. Shebeen Queens bought and sold liquor. They paid so-called "colored" men to go to the liquor stores for them.

The whole business, illegal from start to finish, was fraught with pitfalls. Many a time the runner made away with the money. The more astute shammed arrest and confiscation; and others still just simply came back reeking, having found it more expedient to carry the goods inside their ribs. However, there were trustworthy runners who were reputable and enjoyed a brisk trade.

The police, agents of the government, were hard put to it minding the morals of Africans. It didn't hurt them either that liquor raids were profitable to them (in more ways than one). Bribery: cash, kind, or other kind, welcome currency.

We had arrived in Cape Town the previous Sunday following a two-day journey by train. From Cape Town to Retreat, our final destination, we had taken a local train.

Faces plastered to windows, we were mesmerized by the wonders we saw: what houses, streets, and cars. People, all so many, all so different. Even the mountain here seemed more ... shall I say, mountainy.

The further away the train moved from Cape Town, the less impressive the buildings began to look. From Retreat station we had then walked just less than three miles (I got to know the distance well in later years). When we finally arrived at Blaauvlei, the location where we were to live, a tin shack location, sprawling as far as the eye could see, awaited us.

Here, each shack declared to all and sundry that it had nothing to do with any other shack. Such was the complete lack of coordination in whatever one could care to think of; position, color, structure; you name it, it was different for each of the hundreds and hundreds of shacks. Such individualism would have been hard to design.

All the shacks were made of corrugated iron (zinc) sheets nailed on thin poles and, inside, covered with cardboard boxes that had once contained merchandise from unknown manufacturers, and had been opened and flattened for such use. The cardboard was then plastered over with newspaper. One needed a lot of starch or flour to make the paste used in papering. Unfortunately, mice adore the taste of both starch and flour; certainly to judge from the ceaseless gnawing; day, night, and any other time in between; it was rarely quiet.

Despite the glaring gap between the expectations I had harbored and the far from swanky reality that was my new life, the bubble didn't burst. The belief that our situation had improved tremendously persisted despite very strong evidence to the contrary. Mere proximity to the splendor of the city mesmerized me with promise of attainability.

I do not remember how many rooms the first house we moved into had. I do not even know whether I ever saw the other rooms. We rented one room, a back room, a damp room, from the family who owned the house and who lived in the front part.

This family looked, sounded, and smelled as if they had seen better days. They must have, because the ones they were seeing, when I came to know them, could not have been worse. Except that when I saw them again, some twenty-five years later, hard though this would have been to imagine when we lived in their house, they actually were faring worse. I guess even in reaching rock bottom, there are different levels of bottom and different hardnesses of rock.

Our landlords lived on the principle contained in the location saying; "Friday! Pay day! Fight day!"

Laborers in South Africa are usually paid by the week; the most popular pay day being Friday. I suppose because for most employers, that is the last full work-day of the week, Saturday being a half work-day, and Sunday, bless the dear country that puts "God first" in its constitution, is usually not a work-day.

In this family, there was mother, father, two brothers, and Nomabhelu, the little girl who was about my age.

We did not lodge long with them. My dear father, a lay preacher of the Anglican Church, did not relish his innocents being exposed to the language the Masola family was wont to use, especially Friday nights.

On these nights, Mr. Masola would return from work already drunk. His wife, none too sober herself, would have been sopping booze, day long, from Shebeen Queens. Her familiar currency, "As soon as Nomabhelu's father comes home, I'll send her to you with your little something," she would risk death to honor.

The squabbles, over money that he had squandered on liquor, and money that he refused to give her for groceries for fear she would squander it on liquor, often ended in full-scale fights, with one or both spouses bleeding, swearing, or out cold.

The children in this family did not attend school although the boys were of school-going age. In the vicinity of our landlord's doorway, there was an ever-present pungent smell; the children were invariably in ragged dirty clothing; hair uncombed, and legs announcing a need for a good scrubbing.

The Masolas had long learnt how to fend for themselves. Often, children and mother would come to our door begging for food. This practice exasperated my father who was not consoled by mother's generosity, rightly pointing out we were paying this family rent, and for a room where, when we were having a meal, we had to hold newspaper over the dishes as otherwise the particles of sand that ceaselessly sifted through the leaky unceilinged roof peppered the food.

Although such conditions cannot be escaped soon enough, we did move, within the first year, to another one room in another part of the location. This room was not only cleaner, but it was also in a building where the other tenants were clean, decent, church people whose children attended school.

We gave our grateful thanks to God, ecstatic we had moved to a better room in the same lavatoryless slum: completely overlooking that we would still, daily, risk wet human dung, like congealing paint, seeping through between our toes as dough through a kneader's fingers, covering our bare feet, to leave a smell that would cling long after we had rid ourselves of the tar.

I have very fond memories of our home at Solomon's (for that was the name of that part of Blaauvlei). My first day of school is linked to this home; some of my childhood friends with whom I am still in touch today, belong to this era. Siziwe, our beloved sister, died and was buried from this house. She died during my first year of school. I was still too young to grasp the meaning of the event fully. But I know that was the very first time I saw my father cry. And, although I didn't know exactly why, that made me also cry.

It is here, too, I learned to read my first word — VASELINE!

4

What then, of my childhood, child of the child of my child? Was it happy? Poverty ridden? Or plagued with trauma, crime, illness, or some other malady?

No! To my child eyes, my childhood was stable and happy. It had a reasonable mix of tragedies, both minor and major.

My parents loved us, there was no doubt about that, most of the time. Their idea of raising children, however, was simple, direct, and innocent of ameliorating influence of any theory — psychological, sociological, anthropological, or any other such profundity. They were

staunch adherents of the adage, "spare the rod and spoil the child."
Often, a neighbor would intervene. A practice from which we learned
to throw our embarrassment to the wind, screaming as loudly as we
could, as soon as the beating began.

Corporal punishment was common practice when we were children. We got it at home, at school, and even at church on occasion.
Therefore, we didn't take exception to it — which is not to say we
liked it. Father, a man of very few and rather gruff words, would
sometimes explain to us that such punishment was one of the ways
parents showed their love for their children. Any child who was allowed to grow wild and was never punished for doing wrong was not
as loved as we were and, upon reaching adulthood, would not know
any better and would always be in trouble with the law, with other
people, and worse, possibly even with God. We wailed often, for we
were much loved.

If one word could summarize the kind of childhood I had, "ordinary" would probably be that word.

Then, I had no idea of the link between the color of my skin and
the difference in lifestyles; between mine and those of children of a
lighter hue, "coloreds," and those of a yet lighter shade, whites. The
axiom, "white best, colored next, and black worst" was not yet in my
ken. In fact, at that stage of my life, I had great difficulty identifying
color in people: for years, my eyes saw no significant difference between Indians, coloreds, or whites. Did they not all have long silky
hair?

Although I can swear by all that is sacred that not a penny was ever
spent on a toy by my family, we children were never at a loss as to
what to do with ourselves. We played in groups, usually with both
girls and boys participating.

A good deal of my waking day, I spent in happy play: there were
games played by girls only and games for boys only. But when there
was a shortage, a girl could find herself treated as an honorary boy,
as long as there was need of an extra player; and boys sometimes,
though rarely, deigned to play some girls' game. Of course, there
were girls' games no self-respecting boy would even think of taking
part in.

Any toys that came our way did so by way of charity: organizations such as the Cape Flats Distress Association (CAFDA) gave Christmas parties for children living in the locations.

We went to these parties for two reasons and two reasons only: to get toys; to fill ourselves with the cakes, pies, cold drinks, and sweets — things never on the grocery list in our homes. In fact, what list am I talking about? The parties were publicized via the location link — if one child knew, we all knew.

We did not question why it was that the beneficent were invariably white, the beneficiaries invariably black. We had no way of knowing about the broader issues that had given birth to the organization itself, let alone understand its mission, to say nothing of the inadequacy and limitedness of its undertaking. How were we to know that many of these kind ladies were the wives and daughters of the men who paid our fathers peanuts; fed their dogs T-bone steak; and ensured our poverty by voting in a government whose avowed task was making certain we would stay servants, serf-like and docile? We were children. That these ladies were from another world, that they were giving us their time, showing us their Christian caring, alleviating our poverty, if for one day in a year, was completely lost on us: we did not even know we were poor.

Another source of toys was the white world where almost all the working women of my childhood were employed as nannies, housemaids, chars, and cooks. These women brought, into the black locations, droppings off the white families they served. They returned with bags bulging with cold toast, stale bread, molding cheese, milk, cake, and whatever other food was threatening to go off despite refrigeration. They came back with clothing — shoes, socks, hats, underwear, sweaters, dresses, raincoats, coats, gloves, blouses, skirts, pants, and anything else one can imagine, in various states of disrepair. Those who worked for families with children also brought toys to their homes. Books and comics were another offering.

Those of us who had working mothers, aunts, sisters, neighbors, or family friends would run to welcome them long before they were anywhere near their destination, their houses. They would be forced to tell us what they had brought us from work. Those women who had stingy madams were forced to buy some delicacy such as fruit, sweets, or meat on their way home.

Whatever their own family composition, not one of those women was stupid enough ever to tell an employer they had no use for any gift. If one didn't have a child who could use a toy, a doll, a train, a dress, a slice of bread, a piece of cheese, a book, a pair of shoes, a raincoat, a comic book, old newspaper, or whatever else was being thrown out, one had enough sense to know there were scores of children and adults who could use anything, whatever state it was in.

So great was the need.

My own initial contact with the world of English books and comics was greatly aided by a white family I would never know: a neighbor, Mrs. Waya, would bring these, among other goodies, from her place of employment. There must, therefore, have been children my age in that family. Thus did I get introduced to characters such as Billy Bunter, his equally fat sister, Bessie, Roxanne and a host of other characters from *The Girls' Crystal* and *The School Friend*. Mickey Mouse, Minnie, Goofy, Scrooge, Donald Duck, Popeye and his sweetheart, Olive; Nancy, Sylvester and Puddy Tat, and even Bob Hope, I also met. Blondie and Dagwood are childhood friends I have passed on to my own children. I envy them their perpetual youthfulness.

Whilst I can vouch for the innocence of my family regarding buying any reading material, even the daily newspaper, I read books, granted mostly with limited comprehension. *Pride and Prejudice, Cry the Beloved Country, Great Expectations, Lorna Doone, Alice in Wonderland, Treasure Island*, are some of the spoils Mrs. Waya threw our way.

Nearly all the books and comics she brought were in good repair. However, I remember a few times, it did happen that I would be engrossed in a story only to have to stop short of experiencing the thrill of getting to the end because there were pages missing. Later, I learnt to make up my own endings.

Of my childhood friends, only Dawn had such things as nighties, shoes, socks, and other not strictly necessary items of clothing. Years later, a group of us, comparing notes as adults, realized that those of

24

us who, as children, had such things, had had mothers who were domestic workers.

Aunt Maria used to come to our home on Thursdays, her day off. With her own family a long way away in some remote rural area, she had adopted us as her family away from home. What did she not bring us! Pudding, toast, some clothing, fruit, and other gems.

I had occasion to recall Aunt Maria many many years later. My three children, beginning to be vocal about their deprivation, had appointed the youngest, Sandile:

"Sisi, can you tell us why you cannot have a nice job like the other children's mothers?"

A little puzzled, for although I was a humble schoolteacher, none of the other mothers in our street were brain surgeons either, I explained the job I was doing was very necessary to children as without it they would grow up ignorant. When I wanted to know what job they had in mind for me the prompt answer came from the most forward, the middle child, Thokozile:

"A job that gives you nice things to bring us. Look at the other children! Their mothers bring them cakes, cheese, cold meats, dolls . . ."

Thembeka, not to be left out, made the most telling observation, as befits the eldest:

"Sisi, your job is boring!"

The consensus was that my teaching job was altogether unattractive. I didn't blame the kids. The only thing I ever brought home from work was work to grade! Hidden benefits such as not being threatened with notices of eviction, every other month, thanks to my unpretentious teacher's salary, did not begin to compare, to my offspring, with the tangible, visible, and heavenly goodies other mothers brought their children.

5

I had been as blind when I was a child. Our parents had faced a grim reality we knew nothing about. Mother, at some time or another, has sold sweets, vegetables, *vetkoek*, sheep-head, sheep-trotters, homemade ginger beer, cigarettes: all this illegally as she did not have a permit for selling anything from her home. On occasion, she has sold kaffir beer, *skokiaan*, and hard liquor; these illegal twice over: not only did she not have a license to sell them, but possession, by an African, of these substances, was illegal at the time. She has undertaken sewing, knitting, and domestic work as a way of earning some money. Never, in my mind, were any of these activities linked to father's wages: it was enough, for me, to know that father worked and got paid on Fridays.

Poverty datum line, making ends meet, cheap or uncivilized labor and exploitation; all these were concepts as foreign to me then as the language of the Martians is to me now. Organizations such as the Black Sash were compiling statistics about the plight of the disenfranchised in South Africa. I've often wondered whether some of the ladies of the Christmas parties were also Black Sash members. Whatever the answer, even then, there were souls, white souls, who were perturbed by the treatment the darker races of the land were receiving. And such alarm had been voiced even before the first white foot stepped onto shore from the floating house that had been blown there (surely, by an ill-wind!) in 1652.

Ntsikane, a Xhosa Seer, had predicted the enslavement of the African at the hands of white people. 1948 saw the sealing of that struggle: the Afrikaner became absolute rulers. From then on, systematically, the African would be stripped of whatever little remained of what had once been his own.

We played cops and robbers and identified completely with cops, the good guys of comic and cinema myth. In our own lives, however, cops were feared, disliked, regarded with suspicion, the known enemy of our world. Cops caught our parents, our relatives, and our neighbors for what appeared to us children as everything. Cops were bad luck. Cops were the only arm of government we experienced. And cops took people to jail.

To ward off misfortune — evil spirits, bewitching by another, job loss, cops and arrest — our parents lived by charms, herbs, and witchdoctor forecasts.

When charms, herbs, incisions, prayer, and whatever other means of coping and protection had been enlisted failed, common sense prevailed. Once, mother became aware a liquor raid was upon her, a house or two away. She grabbed the aluminum tub that hung on a bent nail behind the door; onto the floor it went, into it went the water we kept in a four-gallon tin, into the water mother.

The first policeman who barged in let out a howl: *"Here God, die vroumens is kaal!"* (Good God, this woman is naked!), as he beat a hasty retreat, the others doing a right about turn without bothering to enter.

A nakedly pregnant black woman had, obviously, been the last thing these gentlemen expected. And for such an escape, what was the family's entire supply of water?

Sacrifice was also called for when visitors were expected. Our eyes preceded theirs and saw what they would see: the uneven legs of the table; the cupboard door stuffed with rags so it could close; newspaper tablecloths and cupboard liners; the hasn't-been-polished-since-last-Christmas floor; all these and more, suddenly lay naked to our eyes, stripped of their comforting familiarity. Floor polish was not something one bought as a matter of course; there had to be a very good reason for that, the visit of some august person; an elder, the minister, or a teacher.

None of these people, however, provoked the frantic and frenzied cleaning that the doctor did. His stature was enhanced in our eyes by the fact that he was white.

A doctor's visit provoked a veritable panic attack! "He'll take one look at the house," we told ourselves, "and pronounce: 'No wonder you people are always sick. Look at this filth! You should all be dead, living like pigs!'"

To escape the condemnation we felt we richly deserved, the floor was scrubbed and polished, windows opened wide, sheets, night-dresses or pajamas, and anything else we thought would help us hide our poverty from him, borrowed.

It was absolutely imperative, therefore, that knowledge of who had sheets, tablecloths, towels, wash-basins, night-dresses and usable dishes be at the fingertips of all, the same way people elsewhere keep a list of all emergency telephone numbers.

Calling the doctor was a last resort: a frightful nuisance and expensive. It is understandable, therefore, that doctors were called only when it became obvious that a death certificate would soon be needed.

If anything frightened the community more than death itself, it was a certificateless death. Perhaps nowhere is the cultural difference, between African and white, more marked than in dealing with death: having to answer numerous hostile questions about the deceased is not our idea of mourning.

So, a doctor's visit, more often than not, spelled death literally. And "we've sent for a doctor" had the same effect as the tolling of the bell I was to hear about in English poetry: no bell tolls in the townships.

The restless Mediterranean-summer days drove us out of doors, away from mothers and away from chores. Outside, the problem was which pleasure to pursue. We swam dams, climbed hills, milked goats that were not ours, directly into our mouths, harvested vegetable gardens we had not planted, hunted rabbits of the veld and birds of the forest, played dolls' house, played weddings, church, school (I am at a loss now to explain this death wish — we all hated school but that didn't stop us, apparently, from missing it during vacation), and a host of other games, pranks, and mischief besides.

Those greedy days! Instead of exhausting us because of their length and the vigor with which we hurled ourselves into them in earnest play, they only whetted our appetites.

We would walk half a day to get to the azure waters of Muizenberg. We braved streets and motor cars, a railway line, colored residential areas, white neighborhoods, long winding lanes on steadily rising terrain, the vineyards of Constantia and Tokai, our prize. There we would glean boxfuls of hanepoort, the sweetest grape in the whole wide world, pay six-pence or a shilling a box, and set off to Blaauvlei with our entrepreneurial spirits soaring: the loads on our heads gladdening our hearts, making us light-footed.

With reluctance did we respond to our mothers' evening calls. More often than not, we had to be forcibly dragged indoors and to the chores, dull chores that did not begin to compare with the clamor, glamor, and excitement of play.

Then there were the all-too-short winter days when playtime was stolen by the wicked rain that brought near havoc to our lives, mothers having designated it hazardous to the health of children at play.

For it did not stop them from sending us to school, to the shop, or to a neighbor. Who needs to be protected against playing, rain notwithstanding?

Winter was fraught with danger. The cold, clammy, dank and dark shacks we lived in seemed to intensify whatever weather prevailed: ovens in summer; fridges in winter. For heat, we used coal. An inexpensive way to obtain this commodity was to pick coal along the railway tracks. This would be what had dropped from the goods-trains fueled by coal. Of course, this was dangerous. But that was the least of our concerns; it was also illegal to enter the tracks. We were trespassing. I had never even heard the words "beating the system," but doing something that I could be arrested for, for a reason I couldn't and didn't bother to fathom, had a definite allure for me. It never entered my (even then) thick skull that the fine my parents would have to pay would be a tragic setback.

Greater danger, however, came from this same source of heat. No, not the burns which are part and parcel of such means of heating. Among blacks, carbon monoxide poisoning is as constant a threat as drowning in white homes where swimming pools abound. In swimming-pool drownings the casualties are usually little children; carbon monoxide poisoning does not discriminate: it has happened that whole families have been discovered ice-cold in the morning, victims of their attempts to keep from freezing to death.

Everyone knew that the brazier had to be taken out of the house before people went to bed. Unfortunately, many were seduced by the prospect of warmth throughout the night.

Our carefree, fun-filled days were punctuated by adult demands. The city chores were different from those I had been in the process of learning in the village. My brother often in fact fell foul of our parents because of his great reluctance to do housework. Mother and father explained there would be no more male or female tasks in Cape Town as there were no cattle for boys to herd. Thus, we were expected to take turns doing dishes, fetching water, and performing other household chores.

Floors, in the mud hut of the village, are smoothed bare earth. To keep the dust down, they are smeared with cow-dung, fresh cow-dung. This keeps the floor clean, green, and gives the room a fresh smell. In the tin shacks of the location, the floors are made of wood. I now scrubbed and, occasionally, even polished floors.

Where I had fetched water from the river, I learned to open and shut taps. We did not have running water in the house though. There was a communal tap. So I had to fetch water and, since we paid for the water here, I had to learn, very early, to carry a four-gallon can on my head. I learned to cook on a primus stove, using kerosene for fuel and methylated spirits to kindle it. In the village we had gathered twigs for kindling and wood and dry cow dung had been our fuel. I, certainly, had come a long way!

So fast was the pace, agility of mind had to be matched by nimbleness of fingers as fleas replaced lice in the daily onslaught on our bodies. Funds permitting, we bought DDT to strengthen our defense.

I learnt about products such as Vim, for scouring pots and pans. Our own Vim though, in the location, was ash and sand. I learnt to mind younger children; mother was to have five more children in Cape Town. I learnt these and many other time-consuming, petty, little, and annoying tasks without which, I am sure, families would perish and civilizations crumble! These tasks were learnt, practiced, and perfected, to the best of my youthful abilities and reluctant inclination. This is not to say I was never assailed with bouts of self-importance, as occasionally happened, when an adult gave praise for a job well done or when one's superior skills outshone another's. Such evidence of one's maturity would then be accompanied by a startled period of being a model child. Mercifully, that was short-lived.

Our home became a home from home for people from our village (called our homeboys and homegirls) who had been excised from their own families by the combined exigencies of their need for employment and the government's influx control policy, a policy aimed at keeping Africans away from the urban areas of South Africa. A policy that succeeded in wrecking African families. Arriving, they brought letters and messages for the other migrants and, returning, they took back money, letters, messages, clothing, and medicine from this same group to the families in the villages. My home was a veritable gateway.

Like these migrant laborers, father had lived in bachelor quarters before his family came to join him. Now that he had a home, he also had a duty to his former "roommates."

As we ourselves lived in a single room in the beginning, a room that was bedroom at night, living-cum-dining room during the day, a bathroom and anything else room, any addition meant over-over-crowding. But we did what had to be done. Our visitors slept where we slept and ate what we ate.

Brides also came to get married to sweethearts whose contracts stretched months longer than their patience, threatening to put asunder that which burned to be together. Bhuti Phuphu, a bachelor, brought the young woman he was about to marry to our house. Living under a lay preacher's roof, she would qualify for a church wedding, whereas, had the groom-to-be taken her to his rooms at the hotel, where he worked, the church would have refused to marry them.

Mzoxolo, Mandla's younger brother, took ill and his mother, Aunt Makhwange, brought him to Cape Town to be near his father and near good doctors. Uncle Dyantyi would come to be with them every Sunday, his day off. And they stayed with us until Mzoxolo's health had been restored.

Occasionally, migrants were forcibly packed home: fears that they were becoming too attached to the women with whom they had liaisons in the city prompted such action. That kind of affair was not supposed to make one forget one's wife back home. Once, when such a person was being sent home, something got out of hand. I never got to know exactly what. Anyway, there I was, sound asleep when I was awakened by the noise of men at war.

Frightened, I sprang up crying. And at just that second, a blow aimed at another was deflected and the front end of the stick pierced my right thigh. To this day, I bear witness to that fight two inches above the right knee.

Fights were not usual, though, when the going home was voluntary. It was the fact that a man was being sent home in disgrace, as it were, that inevitably caused blood to flow. That, and the home-brewed beer that, to amaXhosa, is part and parcel of any group activity.

Another group that went home through no will of their own were the truly and verily departed:

It is a Sunday morning: "*Nkqo! Nkqo-nkqo!* Is this the home of

31

Tolo from Umtata?" a voice asks. We freeze. Strangers in the location can spell big trouble.

"Who wants to know?" father responds, going to the door. He opens it. Two men, strange men, stand awaiting admission. "Come in. Where are the strangers from?"

"We are from Sea Point."

"Yes?"

"Well, that is all."

"I see." And almost as an afterthought, "Are you passing by or should the child get a chair next door?"

"We will be here a while," reply the strangers.

"Sindiwe, go and borrow a *bankie* (bench) next door."

When I returned the older of the two men was saying, "He became cold; there and then. Cold. Now the police want a relative to come to the *mopp* (morgue) and point him out. That is why we are here."

Tata then turned to us, to mother and to us children and relayed the news of the death of his cousin Sondlo.

Dear Bhuti Sondlo was no more. Felled by a hit-and-run car the night before. His wife and their four sons were, respectively, minus husband and father. The champion of *iintsomi* and tongue-twisters (the longest tongue-twister, according to the Guinness Book of Records, is the Xhosa one that goes, *"Iqaqa laseQawukeni laqabela entabeni, laziqikaqika kuqaqaqa, laza laqhawuka uqhoqhoqho!** and I had learnt it from him). The master teaser lay silent. Never again (enjoying his day off) would he tell bare-footed snot-nosed children reluctantly getting ready for school on a wintry morning, thick frost scrunchily shiny on the ground:

"Sleep! Is there anything more glorious on earth?

The poor, like the rich, get it.

The ugly, as the beautiful, enjoy it.

You, now, have to leave it and go to learn!

While I, like a king, remain under the blankets!"

---

* *The skunk of Qawukeni went up the mountain, rolled itself over and over on the grass, and then his windpipe broke.*

His family would have had a very hard time. But his boss took on 16-year-old Simphiwe, Sondlo's eldest son, as replacement. Most African workers have no insurance, at work or privately, and Sondlo had been no exception.

In all this human activity, I, as a child, was an observer, a minor participant, at most; a child looking on and watching adults doing adult things.

Growing up

"*U kafile ngunyoko!*" ("Your mother is a kaffir!"). On my way to the clinic near the railway line between the two stations of Retreat and Steenberg, I heard those words said with hot anger, rare in my mother, who lost her temper every so often but seldom was angry. She startled me. I do not know what impact, if any, the words had on the fast-receding figure on a bicycle, of a young colored man who had provoked them: "Kaffir!" he had hissed, riding past.

Besides this verbal outburst, I saw and heard little else by way of reaction from my mother. However, my whole being sensed her changed mood: Anger? Pain? Hatred? Or frustration? Something, I didn't know what, flowed wordlessly from her: I did not know all these words then, but I knew she was a different person from the one with whom I had stepped out of the house such a short while ago.

Where before she had been cheerfully pointing out shrubs, plants, and trees that reminded her of Gungululu where she was born and where she grew up, she now walked with resolute earnestness, tight-lipped. Now, we seemed bent on getting to the clinic and, once there, getting immunization, for which I was being taken, over and done with as quickly as possible, so that we could retreat to the relative haven of our location, Blaauvlei.

Blaauvlei! When I think of my growing up, Blaauvlei seems to be where it took place. I lived there for a total of three years, now that I look back. But the vastness of it, its vibrancy, throbbing aliveness, and its many-faceted complexity make those three years seem much longer. The filth, squalor, poverty, shabbiness, sharpened one's senses. You knew who you were in Blaauvlei. You had to know who you were just as surely as skin enveloped your body. The you you knew you to be was a vital protection against an environment where private hope was a tenuous ailing plant:

"He sank in the sand!" or, "The sand swallowed him!" Said of those whom the insatiable environment got the better of; those who, like the pigs that wallowed in the stagnant, garbage-filled, vermin-infested ditches that pockmarked Blaauvlei, became indistinguishable from it.

Blaauvlei sprawled proudly in a splendid ocean of tin shacks, or *pondoks* as we called them. I was very happy there. Each *pondok*, each humble structure of wood, zinc, cardboard, and paper artistically held together by nail, starch, rope, wire, and determination, bespoke poverty. But it also proclaimed the will to be. I was a child, happy in the knowledge of the love of my parents and brother.

I can still see the location, Blaauvlei. The best picture I have to this day, and one I can recall with remarkable facility, is the view from the hill: I am coming from school. Up Boundary Road, running. At the foot of the hill the tarred road comes to an abrupt end. With my back to the avenues, tarred roads, street lights, brick houses with individually enclosed yards, I begin the demarcating climb. The ancient white hill, God-made, watches the man-made tarred road, the broad black belt, at its feet. Like a sentinel, the scrub-dotted hill stands silently surveying all around it.

Progress this side along the banks of Boundary Road and on the other side, deliberate and designed retardation. This side, poor-white people and far-from-poor colored people lived. On the other side black people, Africans, lived. And they were all poor, so poor they could never understand how the label applied to white people living in houses with electricity.

Through years of usage the hill had been eroded at this point so that where Boundary Road stops the hill dips, yielding a passageway. Still running, up, up, up the hill I go, the sand washing through between my toes. As I reach the top, roofs fly into my eye; some pitched, others flat, some painted, but most sporting the natural reddish brown of well-worn zinc. And then, to the right, the beckoning dam! All this is bordered, far, far into the horizon by gentle white sandy hills, the barren dunes dotted with shrub, that are a distinct feature of the Cape Flats.

Blaauvlei stretches as far as the eye can see; far, far away towards Steenberg. But it is the dam that gives me back my breath: glistening temptress on warm days and Discoveryland when swimming wasn't uppermost in our minds. I still can't understand why the spirogyra became such a formidable foe in high school. What fun only yesterday! Touching, smelling, and tasting the unknown, the mysterious, and the forbidden? Come to think of it, like the American Indian on a postcard, the only spirogyra I ever met in high school was a diagram; safely tucked in between the pages of a textbook: no longer living, interesting, or interested.

School, someone has said, is where learning stops. How sad; how very true.

2

"Pick-pick, mama!"

"Pick-pick, Miss Nomsa!"

"Pick-pick, Sis' Lindiwe!"

"Pick-pick, *umlungu!*" (a white person)

In this game of oneupmanship, the caller "picks" someone admired. Picking was tantamount to wishing to be that person. The competitor, in response, picks another person, even better. The winner was the caller who could show the superiority of his or her choice.

"If I am a white person, I have everything. I am rich. I have a big house. I drive a big car. In fact, I don't even drive it myself. That's how rich I am; I have servants to do as I please!"

Perhaps children in other lands played at being kings and queens; we just played at being white.

What I heard and what I saw were what I heard and what I saw. I was a child and saw with the eyes of a child.

Aspects of the environment that appeared as steadfast, unchanging givens that order the world in which there is the sun by day and the moon by night, are taken as truth; no doubt admitted.

Such was the clarity of my vision that, although now, when I think back, I cannot recall anyone ever telling me that whites were better (not in the same way I had been given instructions about the omnipotence, omnipresence, and omniscience of the Deity), I know that by the time I reached my teens, that fact was firmly, unshakeably, rooted deep in my mind.

Who can wonder? The whole environment screamed: "WHITE IS BEST!"

Who drove cars? Whites. Who wrote books? Whites. Who owned shops? Whites. Who lived in houses as distinct from shacks? Whites. Who always wore Sunday-best Monday through to Monday? Whose children always wore shoes to school? Who bought toys? Who bought butter? And the lovely négligées so tantalizingly displayed at the windows of the never-dreamt-of-being-entered-by-me shops such as Stuttafords? Who sat at table for meals? Who had meals to sit at table for and tables to sit at? Who had servants and who were never servants? Who rode the first-class coaches of the trains? Whose babies were pushed around in perambulators by uniformed nannies? Who had nannies who saw their kids to and from school, helping them cross busy streets? Guess whose children were fending for themselves? Who, as adults, had leisure time and leisure to pursue? Who could wear any color clothes and not be petrified they would soil at the beginning of their sweaty day? Guess who didn't have sweaty days, unless, by choice, they sweated at play! Who had washing machines, toasters, polishers, swimming pools, electricity in all their homes; running water too? Hot water? Bathrooms? Toilets inside every home? In all their homes?

Mama and Tata were very ordinary in any way you care to think.

Neither of them had completed primary school. They did not have any money. Neither had any ambition, for themselves, to get involved in any of the community organizations. The exception was the church. Much as they valued education and were keen on us children going to school, they were not interested even in the school committees. Father's outlook which he sometimes voiced, was, "There's so-and-so who is dying for the honor. Let him have it."

My parents were far from remarkable. They were, indeed, ordinary to the point where it sometimes hurt. There were times I thought I would never forgive them that very ordinariness. Estelle's mother was a volunteer, as members of the African National Congress were called then. These women would go around the whole of the vastness of Blaauvlei singing, boldly:

"*Andiyoyik'intwazan'engangam*   "I do not fear a little
Andiyoyik'intwazan'engangam   girl like me. Even should
Nokub'ingakhula, ikhul'ibe   she grow and grow to be
ngangam!"   as I am!"

Voicing their fearlessness!

They were protesting against, among other things, the pass laws. How I envied Estelle such a mother.

On the rare occasion someone, never one of us children, brought up father's lack of engagement in any of these community activities except the church, that gentleman of scarce smiles would reply, "My friend, I am hard put to it remaining human, maintaining and conducting myself as a person, getting up each day, going to work, bringing the pay packet home on pay days, cherishing my spouse, respecting my neighbor, refraining from crime, and, above all, remaining intact mentally."

My parents did all these things and even worshipped God on Sundays and tried to keep His law every day.

Of course, as a child I was not altogether satisfied with this. However, although there were a few times when I was sorely tempted to trade in my parents for others, I never quite came to the point of embarking on this project.

By standard six, the last class of primary school, I had an impressive vocabulary in the English language, then the only medium of instruction in African schools. However, I do not recall greater joy than that experienced when learning my very first English word: the process is as vivid in my mind today, nearly four decades later, as if it were yesterday. Picture the single room — bed, dining, bath, living, and everything else — the all-purpose room we call home. Mother, father, brother, younger sister, and I, then the middle child.

The walls are papered. Not your usual wallpaper; oh no, sir! The daily newspaper, bought by some unknown white family and no doubt carted by same family's servant to the location, had finally found its way to our home. Many are the uses we found for newspaper: toilet paper, window-cleaner, carpet, cupboard-liner, and wallpaper. In my home, however, it had to be a teaching aid too.

My brother, the eldest child, school-going, just had to share his vast store of newly acquired knowledge. VASELINE: Phonetically, the word was taught to me, pronounced as in Xhosa, our mother tongue, VARCERLINAH!

Yes, even in Blaauvlei, the intended function of the newspaper was performed, if by chance!

3

My horizon widened as I grew older. Mine was the intoxication of the erstwhile chrysalis finding herself a free, bewinged, fearlessly roaming creature of flight, darting here, there, everywhere; no longer immobilized by her very physique. O-o-oh, Blessed Joy! I went, alone, to the location shop. I was sent to the neighbors in the evening alone. I was left alone minding the pot cooking on the primus stove. Later, but soon enough, came school with its rituals, regulated playtime, and the use of the other name given at baptism — the school name or Christian name. For the first time in my short life, I answered to the name Cynthia. And later still, I was trusted with the adult task of going, by train, by myself to Wynberg.

Wynberg is a white suburb with reasonable shopping and cannot be more than five or so miles from Retreat, where I caught the train. I was in real danger of bursting apart with pride and feelings of importance, the first time mother sent me there. The fact that I had been sent to buy such lowly articles as buttons, elastic, and a baby bottle in no way detracted from the impressiveness of the feat I had been called upon to perform and to which I felt more than equal.

With privilege comes responsibility, I was soon to learn. And mishaps are the shadow of every good fortune. Living, as we did, in cardboard, wood, and zinc shacks, fire was a constant specter in our lives. Although my own family has lived in four shacks, we have experienced fire only once. That was one of the luckiest days of my life. Or so it seemed to me that fateful evening. As well, it should have looked as though God Himself had decided to intervene personally in my affairs; for I was absolutely convinced my mother would fulfil a promise of long standing and skin me alive; or worse.

We must have been going through a more than usual stint of austerity. It was during the only period I recall of father being out of a job. One evening, he had walked in from work and instead of the usual greeting said, "*Ndibuya nawo*" ("I return with it"), referring to whatever of the odd assortment of jobs he had done; jobs whose qualification was humility that bordered on self-effacement, zero expectations, and brutelike brawn. His feet would not carry him to that job again. He had "brought it back." That was a less brutal way of saying he had been fired.

My parents did not discuss this development with us children. They never saddled us with whatever pain they were undergoing. Somehow, though, their anxiety seeped through their pores and covered us like the scab of a wound, ugly; hiding raw hurt.

Mother took to putting money in handkerchiefs or rags when sending us to the shop. She would put the money in one corner of the handkerchief, make folds, a knot, and the money was thus secured. For some reason, we found this practice particularly demeaning. We took it as a personal insult. We felt our dignity was at stake, our intelligence in question, our very sense of worth assaulted. I would rather have died than be caught out in this childish practice by a friend. And at that time everyone I knew was a friend and the opinion they held of me mattered terribly. Needless to say, as soon as I was out of mother's sight, I undid the offending knot and carried the money in my very competent hand as any self-respecting, sane person would.

On the day in question, a Friday, I recall vividly, I was sent to get kerosene, which was to be used to cook the evening meal. It was late afternoon. Mother gave me a half-crown and an empty gallon tin. The shop was about a mile away. However, not the physical distance, but the friends I met on the way to the shop were my undoing that day. What with talking, a little harmless playing, running, and laughing, although I swear, all the time my left hand was a tight fist guarding the money, I don't know whatever made me want to verify the presence of the half-crown. I stared at my hand, and what I did not see there, the tightly held half-crown, made my mouth dry.

The hangman's noose would have been a welcome salvation. I kept staring at my hand as if by so doing I could, by some miracle, will the coin back into it. All the steps I had taken. Where could I have lost the money? At what point did it slip out of my hand? These questions raced through my screaming mind as I and a couple of friends retraced my steps, searching for the coin. A hopeless task in view of the fact that we had no roads and the trails we followed, day in day out, were made by the sheer weight of hundreds and hundreds of feet pounding on the sand until footpaths were etched among the sand dunes. What chance of recovering a coin among those trillions of minuscule sand particles whose very texture and behavior combined to defy and undermine one's efforts as well as underscore the futility of those same efforts? Even the saliva test failed. We children believed that dropping saliva on the palm of one hand, hitting it with two of the fingers of the other hand, thus making it fly onto the ground, would pinpoint the direction in which the lost object might be found.

After an hour or so (which probably was far less in reality, but such was my apprehension that it seemed a very long time) had passed between the departure of the little innocent and loved girl from her home and the emergence of the new me who was making, even at that moment, a drastic decision, I concluded I was leaving home. This seemed the wisest choice in view of the certainty I had of my being killed that day by my mother for my deed. How would I explain the disappearance of her money from her well-and-truly-fastened knot? Oh, how clearly, then, I saw the wisdom of her ways.

It grew darker; and as the only decision I had made was that of leaving home, I was somewhat at a loose end. I had no idea where I could go. I knew no one who would welcome me to their home without question, without notifying my parents or dragging me back home. In fact, I was pretty certain to be hauled home by any adult who saw me abroad at this late hour. Such were the disadvantages of living in a small community: not only does everybody know everyone else; they also know everybody else's children and can never keep their noses out of everybody's business, especially when that business is a child. I felt the limitations imposed by my environment with all my heart.

By this time my friends had long left me to my devices, mindful of their own precarious positions with their families, and had gone about their legitimate business. So, hiding from people, I inched my way in the general direction of home. I realized there was a vast difference between the darkness anywhere else and the darkness in the vicinity of my own home: the latter was safer, or so it seemed to me. And, leaving home did not mean I had to be scared out of my mind all night through. I would leave home, but be within my family's earshot in case I were in danger, I reasoned.

It was quite dark by the time I rounded the hill and came within sight of what should have been the darker shapes surrounded by the general dark of a lightless night, the buildings in one of which, in a two-room unit, my family now lived.

However, I was met with the sight of angry, dark, billowing smoke and fiery flames that leapt to the inky sky. The crackling of burning wood was accompanied by shapes of bodies scurrying here, there, and everywhere as people attempted to salvage whatever of their possessions they could lay their hands on; a task made doubly difficult by the presence of scavengers, looters who stood by waiting to steal from the piles rising next to the burning buildings.

Weak with weariness, I ran forward yelling, announcing my presence and safety to my family. Reunion was sweet indeed. My mother had not been able to assure father, or herself, that I had not been sleeping when the fire broke out. To this day, none in my family knows that the copious tears I shed that night had nothing to do with the fact that, except for what I had on, I had no clothes and we had nowhere to call home!

Our situation improved somewhat following the fire, in which, fortunately, no lives were lost. We left Blaauvlei and went to live in a brand-new location, Zwelitsha (New Site). Zwelitsha had been a forest and was cleared specifically for the victims of the fire that had destroyed our home and rendered nearly a hundred persons homeless.

We were given sites on which to build and father put up a two-bedroom house with kitchen and a dining-room. Jongi and I shared the children's bedroom whilst Tata, Mama, and the younger children, a toddler and a baby, shared the other one. Of course, the houses were still shacks but, instead of the customary "building" where as many as twelve families lived in one big tin shack that had been subdivided into smaller units, Zwelitsha was unashamedly pretentious: each house stood on its very own little plot. The houses stood in rows of five. The fifth, much much smaller, stood at a respectfully bigger distance away from the four to its front. It was the toilet, as any who cared to look at its back could easily ascertain from the bucket clearly visible from the hatch. Four families, one toilet; quite an improvement from digging holes in the sand!

4

At school, the teachers said I was a bright pupil. Twice, I was even made to skip a class; I went from Sub B to Standard Two and from Standard Two to Standard Four.

Since in this regard I was following in the footsteps of my idol, Jongi, my joy was therefore doubled. I admired Jongi tremendously. He was nothing if not a hero to me. I read all the books he read. When he joined the Boy Scouts, he taught me some of the things he was learning there: tying a reef knot, the Morse Code, and a few other useful things like that. He was perfection and I proudly paid homage, leading the small troop of his followers, for, among our playmates, he was the undisputed leader. Bright, he was also a very effective stick fighter. As his sister, I basked in his protection.

There were times, though, when I became ambivalent about if not downright resentful of this same protection. A gang of boys who had dropped out of school took it upon themselves to stop pupils from attending. We were the only ones left untouched by what, in my opinion, was a blessing. I also felt the irksome shadow of Jongi's protection when no boy would mess around with me. I was the only girl who had boys as friends, respectful friends and nothing but. Very stern stuff is in my make up: did I even contemplate suicide?

Both Mama and Tata were the second generation in their families to set foot inside a classroom. Mama often regaled us with stories of her youth. Pioneers, I learnt from her, seldom had an easy time. She and a friend had been the subject of much malice in the village when it became known they were "fallen maidens." The demonic deed? They were the first to wear bloomers!

To the village community, where virgins proudly displayed firm breasts, with beaded apron decorously worn over the pubic area, hiding one's body was a sign of shame. What could these two young girls have done to have to *buy* something and have to wear it every day? The collective conscience of the predominantly "red" village wondered.

From very early in life, I was made aware my lot would be much improved were I to go to school and stay there long enough to be something. An almost universally voiced lament by my parents' generation is not having had an education. Most parents, mine amongst these, would attempt to give their children the opportunity they themselves never had. This, at tremendous personal sacrifice.

I had started school at age seven years and five months. The law stipulates that African children start school only after the seventh birthday. White and colored children my age, under no such "protection," were beginning their third year of schooling. Our classes were so overcrowded I could never figure out how the teacher knew everybody's name. I know that until I had been in school at least five full years, and the numbers had thinned considerably, at any given year I probably knew less than a third of my class by name.

We had to buy books and uniforms. We fought a ferocious battle, year long, to safeguard the books we had bought against pilferers. The scourge was rife. Many pupils could not afford the books. Some lost theirs to those who had not bought any; others to those who had had theirs stolen. A book moved at a furious tempo and it was not unusual for a child to see the end of the school year with the third or fourth or worse copy of a book bought at the start of the school year.

I got hooked on school on the last day of my first year there. The whole school was assembled. And there, in that august gathering that included big Standard Six children, almost grown-ups, my teacher read:

"CYNTHIA MAGONA!"

I had passed. I was educable. I was a learned person. The thrill! I ran out of that hall there and then, not waiting for the assembly to finish. My feet were wings as I sped home to mother with the good news. I was to pass many more classes subsequently, but the accompanying joy never quite reached this fervor of that first time.

Despite the unnerving ways of the school, I grew somewhat fond of it. Yes, often of a morning the thought would cross my mind I would be better off not going there. However, staying at home was quite out of the question. Mother was one of those odd parents who not only did not welcome their own little children being home but believed a child should go to school unless going to the doctor. As far as I remember, except for a bout of whooping cough which didn't last long, as a child I was disgustingly healthy. The whooping cough, I had during the school vac.

Another reason for my liking school was the play I was able to pack into the intervals. A morning break; lunch break; and an afternoon break. And at home I played only at mother's pleasure and after I had done my chores.

One day though, I actually played truant. I was in Standard Two, about nine years old. That morning I had not been able to persuade mother to give me the equivalent of five cents. This sum of money was absolutely necessary, in my own mind, for my survival. I did not have three essential articles: a ruler, a pencil, and an eraser. The teacher had warned us she would deal with any child who dared show her or his dirty face in her class the next day without these things.

To appreciate my plight, this beloved lady's method of discipline should be known: if, as we played in our little groupings waiting for the bell marking the beginning of the school day, Miss Mabija was spied wearing a navy skirt and a red blouse, all play stopped. That was her battle dress!

Multiplication tables were hastily revised. So was the spelling list, and the sketchily remembered details from infrequent Scripture lessons. Names of trees. Names of the stations on the Suburban Line, from Cape Town to Simonstown . . . Cape Town, Woodstock, Salt River, Observatory, and . . . and . . . "Hey, what comes after Observatory?"

"Salt River."

"No! Don't be stupid; going to Simonstown."

This frenzied flurry would stop abruptly with the ringing of the bell, when we had to fall into line.

But how does one escape detection for the failure to possess a ruler, a pencil, and an eraser? On my way to school that day the question slowed my feet.

Never one to lay myself on the tracks with an approaching train in full view, I decided to skip school that day. I judged the safest place for me lay somewhere between these two ladies. A little thicket separated from the school by the sandy hillock we called the playground seemed perfect for my needs.

I had a thoroughly awful time. The whole day long, I was in fear of discovery. After morning assembly, I was amazed by the number of dangerous latecomers who ran past, a few feet from my hiding-place. Startling too, was the frequency with which pupils were dispatched hither and thither, like angels of death after my hidden soul.

At such perilous moments, I not only held my breath and remained stock still; I also shut my eyes, crouching.

I don't know what punishment was meted out that day to those without ruler, pencil, and eraser. I do know, however, what this teacher, whom I grew up to admire and be very fond of, was wont to do with culprits:

"Rub-a-dub! Rub-a-dub!" we would recite inching slowly forward, in line, rubbing our seats. As each one's turn came, the culprit knew what to do: touch toes. And the switch would find its mark.

For spelling errors, Miss Mabija had a particularly painful form of punishment: hands, facing palms up with thumbs touching, were put on head. As the lashes fell, the culprit sang, "Let us learn spelling! Let us learn spelling! Let us learn, let us learn, let us learn spelling!"

46

The number of lashes to be received depended on how fast one sang through this ditty. Woe to those frivolous or stupid enough to break down in the middle, interrupting the song: they just had to start all over again. The wise sang it so fast they got away with four or five lashes only.

Another variation on the ordinary manner of giving lashes with a cane on the palm, was making the offender bunch the fingers so that the upper phalanges touched and nails were close together. The thin side of a ruler was then brought down in lashes over the tips of the fingers. The pain that can generate from what must be a diameter of less than half an inch, is unbelievable.

I had my day of playing truant; and I learnt to respect tougher minds who could do, with regularity, what I found so unpleasant that nothing, not mother's meanness nor Miss Mabija's murderous bent, would ever induce me to repeat.

By the end of that most miserable day, I knew whatever could happen to me at school did not compare with the fright to death I had nearly given myself. The threat of being discovered and crawly things, especially snakes, had filled my mind all the time!

When the bell rang at three o'clock, marking the end of the school day, I ran out of my hiding and sped homeward. Not only was I running away from other pupils — they still had prayers and after-school chores such as sweeping the classrooms, raking the school yard — I was eager to get home, for I was famished. Also, I wanted to bury the whole sorry mess of that day. Going home would be the first step towards normalization of my routine.

Relief from school came only during the week's vacation in March and September, three weeks' winter vacation in June, and summer vacation, all of six glorious weeks, in December. This last was the best for more than one reason. It marked the end of the school year. That fact meant we could say goodbye to the teacher we were beginning to weary of and who was getting too familiar with our weaknesses. In January, we would begin a new class with a new teacher. It would be my blessing, however, to have Miss Mabija for two successive years!

5

Six weeks used to be a very long period to me then. We children looked forward to getting up later; not washing ourselves thoroughly; playing more; not having any homework to do; and living free of the fear of the teacher's cane.

And, as if all these good reasons were not enough, this vacation also meant Christmas as well.

Summer in the Western Cape is long, hot, and dry. I always knew when summer was near, the maitland tree wore its yellow blooms. Fluffy flowers, eye-blinding in their colorfulness, vied with the golden-red hot summer sun. The beauty of these trees will forever be wedded in my mind to unbearable anticipation. Heralding, as it did, Christmas!

Christmas was the only time of the year during which we children could look forward, with certainty, to new clothes. For weeks before the day, there was frantic activity in our homes. Houses were painted inside and outside. Plans for the Christmas feast were made; windows that lay broken-paned the whole year through were now mended as parents stretched themselves, even borrowing from employers against future earnings.

This was the time during which furniture shops reaped a bountiful harvest from the unwary customer, who invariably used the hire-purchase or never-never plan (never use it because you'll never get out of it).

As delivery vans from the same company competed for the bonus going to the one that made the most deliveries, companies wrestled bitterly, advertising for the black souls.

We children reveled in the spirit of well-being and expansiveness of the festive season. We looked forward to the only time, in the whole long dreary year, that we were taken shopping. Even the shoes I owned when I was bigger and in the school choir, were always bought for Christmas. That one pair of black "walkers," flat-heeled lace-ups, lasted the whole year through. I wore shoes to school concerts. Those were not numerous in any given year. Not often, I also wore them to church.

On Christmas Day every child wore brand-new "Christmas clothes" and savored "goodwill," little dreaming of the financial stress the custom meant. "Happy! Happy! Happy Christmas!" echoed everywhere. My own personal year stretched, endless and flat, between Christmases.

On Christmas Day father would wake us up long before sunrise. We would then go outside to watch the sun come out "dancing" with glee on the day Baby Jesus was born. We really saw it dance as we watched! But then, we saw sunrise on this day only and no other; who is to say it doesn't dance rising on other days?

With excitement we could barely contain, we would then wash ourselves and get ready for church. Feeling saintlike in our beautiful new clothes that smelled white people's smell, we walked carefully on our way to church, chagrined that most of our friends were still asleep or indoors because it was too early for them to be playing outside. A big part of the excitement of the day lay in the discovery of who wore what and whose what was the prettiest. The secrecy that surrounded Christmas shopping can be likened only to that surrounding arms rivalry between the superpowers. Each of us believed, without the shadow of a doubt, her outfit would be the best, the most exciting. But the curiosity to see what others would be wearing on the big day belied the confidence we purported to possess.

Although, because we went to church service Christmas mornings, our clothes were invariably the first to be seen among those of our own little circle, the consolation, to me was that it was by then too late for anyone to copy or attempt to outdo me. The shops had done their selling and were now closed until two days later, after Boxing Day.

One Christmas, in the midst of the morning's hectic preparations for church, disaster struck. I was in the habit of putting the primus stove between my legs for extra warmth. The morning must have been crisp and, since there was only an iron on the stove, I inched towards it until I was standing, skirt pulled up, with the stove directly underneath.

"What is burning? I smell burning!" Mother and father shouted at the same time to look out. The hem of my dress had caught fire. Quickly, I put out the offender.

My pride, flawed! The dress, a navy taffeta dotted with delicate little white tear-drops, had a full skirt, a perfect circle, a tight bodice with a Peter Pan collar, and short peaked sleeves: it was testimony to the almost miraculous skill of the dressmaker, Mrs. Naidoo, an Indian lady who lived in the avenues, in a real house.

Not only did I suffer the indignity of wearing a dress with a hem from which it looked as if a mouse had taken breakfast; father gave me a beating I would not be in a hurry to forget.

"Sindiwe, how many times have I told you not to roast yourself on the stove?"

Petrified, I looked at him and not a word would croak out of my parched throat. My eyes, in contrast, were brimming.

"What do I have to say to you for you to listen and to understand? Have I or have I not just spent money buying your new clothes? Where, now, is the new dress? Where? Answer me!"

So saying, father asked Jongi to go outside and pluck a switch from a tree.

"And, mind you get a good one or else you'll get it too!" Jongi could never seem to find a good sturdy switch to be used on himself or another of his siblings.

We hardly ever got a hiding if there were visitors or before church. That was one of the very few memories I have of such a thing taking place. I thought I was at death's door before father stopped; and then, only because mother reminded him we would be late for church if we didn't get going.

It was a very subdued butterfly who straggled stoically to church that morning. However, in the nature of childhood maladies, by eating-time, I was back to form; never one to lose my appetite, I was helping, jostling with others and, as mother used to say, going on as if I had been deprived of food for a year.

Besides Christmas and other religious holidays, especially Easter, we had other occasions for feasting, in the course of the year. Of necessarily somber tone, were funerals. As children, we were sheltered from the pain that death brought. Yes, there was sorrow in the air, so to speak, but the gloom I was to smell at these events as an adult, totally escaped us as children. Oh, we knew whoever had been taken by God wouldn't come back. An eventuality which, in my own mind certainly fitted with all those things in which God had a hand.

My understanding of His ways, which I "knew" were not our ways, was that He gave things such as bread and took from us, each night, the souls of those who had died. Since He never took back the bread He gave, it seemed only fair He should keep the souls He took.

As soon as a child could speak, in my father's house, that child was taught the Lord's Prayer. After the evening meal, evening chores, and some family pleasantries, everyone was rounded up for evening prayer. Father's booming voice would announce the hymn to be sung at the onset of prayer. Following the singing, the children standing huddled together, arms folded and eyes closed, would recite the Lord's Prayer.

Afterwards, father or mother, with father's say so, would go into prayer: thanking God for the day and what it had brought us; apologizing for daring to open our unworthy mouths; supplicating for health and safety from all manner of danger; imploring Him to help them look after the children He had lent them; and sending Him to visit the ailing, the poor, those in prison, those at sea, and any we, with our feeble power of remembering, had forgotten. As if this would not keep Him busy enough, He was then asked not to forget our homes, far far away, and the relatives there. "We ask all these things in the name of Him who loved us with a love measureless" — those words were our cue; we would then pipe in, in unison:

"Nkosi, ezandleni zakho,	"Lord, into thy hands
Ndiyawunikel'umoya wam."	I commend my soul."

Many are the times I cheated on that prayer. Why was it we children who commended our souls? Why didn't Ma and Pa commend their souls? So, on occasion I would leave out the possessive adjective, *"wam,"* and, when feeling the world needed improvement, I did not hesitate to commend another's. Of necessity, this was done silently, merely mouthing the name of whomsoever was beneficiary of my prayers that particular night. Remember, I lived in fear of detection. If anyone heard me saying a person's name and if something happened to that person, something bad or worse, would I not then be accused of witchcraft?

I often wondered about the soul. What, exactly, was it? I knew many a part of the body from the slaughtering that often took place.

But the soul eluded me. But then, I had so many other things about which to wonder.

The birth of a baby was another of those things that held tremendous fascination for me. But the abundance that attended this event was always my undoing. So taken up would I be with what unusual foodstuff came into our home and in such hitherto undreamt of quantities, that before I reminded myself I had meant to keep my eyes wide open, the event would be over. The new mother is taken care of by an *impelesi* appointed for that task. This is usually a good friend, a neighbor or a relative, or perhaps a daughter where she is old enough to nurse her mother back to full strength. As mother had six more children after me, spaced carefully three years apart, I was certainly old enough to help with the one directly after me.

Just as babies born into western societies get their BCG before they even leave the maternity hospital, so also were we "fortified" so that we would not fall easy prey to the evil intents of those who wished us ill. Powdery medicine would be mixed with mother's milk and forced down the throat. Other medicine, mixed with oils, would be rubbed on our bodies especially between the eyebrows, on the chest, under the soles of the feet; and then those old enough would be asked, individually, to dip a finger into the can or bottle and rub "down there."

This ritual is repeated each time a new baby comes into the family.

Most traditional medicine is nondescript as far as taste and smell. However, those medicines that do have taste or smell or both, more than make up for any such deficiency on the part of the others.

Vile! Vile and sickening and so terrible I often felt I was in danger of being knocked off just by the foulness of the stench of some of the medicine we had to suffer for our protection. Jongi often had to get a second or third dose because he would bring up whilst taking this kind of medicine. I wisely heeded father's advice and "took it like a man." "Open wide. Swallow hard. It's all over."

Between such medicine and what it was supposed to protect us from, in my opinion we are exceedingly lucky to be here to tell the tale. I also figured if it took such repulsive measures to fight witchcraft, the latter had to be, at least, worse. And that was bad enough for me.

And then there was incision! That certainly beat all other evil, even the corporal punishment that often befell us. Incision was said to be the most potent weapon against witchcraft. *Igqirha*, a witchdoctor, or *ixhwele*, a medicine man, having been invited by father, would appear at our doorstep, unexpectedly for us children. After the chit-chat, during which we vainly hoped he was just passing through, he would begin.

We would be asked to take off all our clothes saving the panties for the girls who were already pubescent. Then he would attack.

Razor in hand, he would take the victim and place him or her facing him. Starting at the top and working his way swiftly downwards, he displays precision many a butcher would envy: again and again the blade slashes. He goes to the fontanelle, two or three little lines each cut into deeply enough not only to open the skin but to draw blood. Often this called for each incision to be repeated: cut-cut, that meant one incision; cut-cut, another. Witchdoctors would make these incisions in patterns of two, or three.

Whatever their fancies dictated, most cut at the fontanelle, then on each temple, the throat, right on the V, where one's chin would fit if the face were flattened and forced back into the neck; then above each breast, down to the abdomen, above the navel and on either side of each knee, above the ankles and, lastly, just above the soles of the feet.

The top and the front done, there was the whole wide-open defenseless back that didn't even have one's tears or grimaces to protect it! The base of the neck is attacked; right above the uppermost vertebra, under each shoulder blade, he goes; cut-cut-cut. Then it is down to the hip joints, away to the outside of both elbows, and onto the outside of each wrist. Between forty and sixty incisions, each cut into at least twice.

The purpose of this whole exercise was not, however, to cut and bleed. Getting medicine into the bloodstream, the objective was then achieved by the direct method: into the raw, open, bleeding incisions, the witchdoctor would rub the jet-black burning powder. His instructions, terse and gruff: "Do not wash for two days" — were given simultaneously to both parents and children. Having been paid, he would depart knowing we would not wash for two days. Our parents would see to that. They were not made of money and were not about to risk calling him back to re-do the job because we had been careless enough to wash the precious medicine off before it had truly taken and penetrated thoroughly into our bloodstream. We, on the other hand, would have stayed unwashed for a year to avoid a repeat demonstration of our parents' concern for our well-being.

In case I have misled you into thinking that this was painful, I apologize. The real ordeal, the ridicule and humiliation, was yet to come. Our special purgatory was the knowing snickers and the jeers, *"Baqatshulwe! Baqatshulwe!"* ("They have been given incisions!") Belonging as we believed we did, in the group of westernized and Christianized people, we were supposed to have left behind all things of darkness: nudity, *imibhaco* (the traditional skirt), red ochre used for cosmetic purposes, and the practice of and belief in witchcraft, to name a few. The practice of ancestral worship was a different matter. The missionaries realized that, if they continued to condemn it, they would empty the Christian Church of its African adherents. We are not easily divorced from our ancestors.

This straddling of two worlds, the world of school and "civilization" and the world of ancestor worship, witchdoctors, and traditional rites, often created disagreements in our home. Following, for example, particularly convincing lessons about fresh air during hygiene classes, one of us would become enthusiastic about "open windows." Well, my mother would rather have died than give witches the opportunity, nay, the invitation to peer into her house while she slumbered defenseless. The benefits of fresh air notwithstanding, she was not a fool, proclaimed my mother, unmoved by our entreaties.

"What do teachers know?" Her stock phrase meant "case closed!"

Even when resourceful Jongi would resort to: "But we are safe. We have been fortified, remember? Remember the witchdoctor?", it was to no avail.

"He didn't fortify you against suicide," mother would retort, adding, "and I didn't send you to school to find out you have a mouth!"

Who could argue against such wisdom?

Illness and death, despite these elaborate protective measures against them as well as other of life's numerous misfortunes, did not stay away from our home and the homes of relatives. Death is another event accompanied by rites and rituals. Rituals we grew up with and value as adults.

The bereaved, notified of a beloved's departure from this life, announce the sad news to neighbors, friends, and relatives, which, at times such as this, could mean anyone within hearing distance.

The subdued tone of voice, deliberately dignified and unhurried movements, the mask-like face of the bearer of the news, often warns the family that the person entering their home does not come with usual or good business.

The women straighten their head-gear, and cover their shoulders with shawl, towel, sweater, or whatever is within reach and will do. The men put on their jackets. And then everyone sits down. Clearly disquieted, those present make a valiant attempt to conduct a normal conversation:

"We are glad to see you."

"Yes, sometimes it is necessary to look up friends."

"How are you, and in what condition did you leave the folk back home?"

"Oh, when I left, barring children's coughs and runny tummies, all was well. And how is everybody in this home?"

"Oh, we got up."

A pause. Then:

"We get a little anxious when friends arrive unexpectedly, and they are from afar."

"Yes, that is natural. Is every adult person present? Or is there someone missing? Shall we wait for . . .?"

"Yes, we are all here. Please tell us . . . you are killing us with the suspense!"

The messenger then, as briefly as possible, narrates the tales of how he came into possession of the news of so-and-so's death. How he has been sent to tell the friends present. How they must not grieve as events of this nature had happened before and would happen again; and again.

Children, who until then would have been scattered around the homestead in play or work, would be summoned by the wailing of the women; so would neighbors.

The nearest neighbors are upon the scene within five minutes of the summons having been sounded. One by one, in little groups and in clusters, they come and hear the story, told over and over as new arrivals make that necessary. Telling people what has brought them together in that home will fall on the shoulders of the oldest man present, the messenger having discharged his duty.

At the principal house of mourning, preparations will begin immediately. The wailing women will be taken by others to another room or, where that is not possible, to a corner in the same room. Here, attempts to quieten them will be made. Other women will busy themselves making tea or coffee — black; for when there is a death in a family, that family is not allowed milk. The men will be clearing a room where, from that moment till the funeral, the vigil will be held.

Once there is a room ready, the women sit there, head-scarves lowered, heads bowed, and shawls, scarves or towels over their shoulders. The chief mourner, wife, mother, or eldest daughter, sits behind the door in total darkness, on a grass mat on the floor. She is covered from head to foot with a blanket. This is also where she will sleep until after the funeral.

For the week or two before the funeral, people will come and go in an endless stream of warmth, support, grief, love, and acceptance of the nature of life and the interdependence of human beings. The bereaved are expected to grieve. They grieve, visibly and long. This is normal, for they have lost someone. They acknowledge the loss and others accept their actions.

This is a time of tremendous freedom for the children who, by the second or third day, have recovered. Because the community takes care of everyday business for the bereaved family, the children are relieved of their chores. They do not even go to school.

From the moment news of the death is announced until the funeral, the bereaved family is, with the help and participation of the community, in prayerful vigil. The mornings are taken up in planning. Who has yet to be notified? Who has indicated they are coming (this, of far-away relatives)? What will be slaughtered on the day of the funeral? Who is paying for what? Who is seeing to what? Have the communal collection papers been ordered? Are they being circulated?

Who will keep track of the money collected? The remaining part of the day is used for preparing for the evening when there will be a prayer meeting, a wake. Black tea or black coffee and unbuttered bread is the fare served at wakes. My people show they are in mourning even by the food they eat.

This dietary austerity will be relieved only after the funeral. On that day, following a lengthy service, first at the home of the deceased and then at church, the coffin is accompanied to the grave and there laid to rest. After hymn-singing, prayer, and sermon, the burial service, all present have to return to the home of the bereaved, this time to "wash hands." Basins of water await those returning from the graveyard; await them outside the gate, for they have to cleanse themselves before they enter this homestead. They wash death off their hands and enter the house pure once more.

Thus cleansed, everyone, including the bereaved, is expected to be of less visibly sorrowful mien. And they should be freer in the manner in which they interact with others. This is in contrast with the somberness that has been imposed on them since the announcement of the death.

The public grieving satisfied, friends, neighbors, and supporters gone, the family now attends to business. Is everyone satisfied at how things were done? What unfinished business remains? Children? Wife? Elderly parents? Who is to shoulder what?

Finally, the big hitherto-unspoken thing comes out — ARE we satisfied at how the deceased died? Or are we going to go to "someone"?

"Someone," in this case, means a witchdoctor, a man or woman professing to be able to see beyond the physical and smell out what mystifies mere mortals.

Irrespective of what is written on the deceased's death certificate, "someone" will etch, as if by red-hot iron rod, another reason and probably blame the death on an individual, a group, or a family . . . not so much by name perhaps as by inference.

When my Aunt Leginah died, this is what happened. A woman, a neighbor, was later implicated.

Aunt Leginah was mother's only sister, precious to her as all only sisters, and indeed all sisters, ought to be. She must have been ten or so years younger than mother, although at the time I thought of mother, married and with four or five children, as much much much older than she was. That Antana (Little Aunt) had just finished her education also helped to confirm my estimate of the age gap between the two sisters. To me then, school and scholarly pursuits were synonymous with children and youth. Mother, having left school years before any of us were born, long before she had married father, belonged to the Stone Age and the times of the Bible.

After her nursing training at Frere Hospital in East London, mother's sister had come to work at the Dr. Stals TB Sanatorium at Westlake, not far from the vineyards of Constantia where, during grape season, we children used to glean. She was a Staff Nurse.

As can be imagined, this appearance in our midst of an educated person, our own blood relative, sent our standing to giddy heights. In our location a professional person was rarer than a hen's tooth.

Antana must have been about twenty-five years old. In contrast to mother's light-skinned beauty, her flawless skin was the color of donga water: a dusky goldness the color of new copper.

She had not been in Cape Town two years when Tat'omkhul' uMarhwanana, my maternal grandfather, took ill. Aunt Leginah took to coming home more evenings per week than was her wont. She lived in the Nurses' Home and usually came to us only on her off-duty days.

Jongi and I noted this development and decided it could mean only one thing: grandfather's illness was grave. That could be the only explanation for Antana's increased frequency of visits. We had no phones in Zwelitsha. Therefore, she needed to come over physically for the councils the grown-ups held once we were out of the way, in bed.

"Grandfather is dying," the oracle, Jongi, enlightened me one morning on our way to school. I believed him. This upgrading of our grandfather's status seemed to make sense. Only severe illness could account for the goings-on in our house. Severe illness that had deteriorated. And, soon thereafter, mother left for Gungululu, the village where she was born and where her father lived. This, of course, proved we had been right in our suspicions.

It was while mother was away that Antana suddenly took ill: One — two — three and she was dead. It happened so fast that before mother got father's letter telling her Antana was at Groote Schuur Hospital with double pneumonia, the telegram reached her notifying her of Antana's death.

We children had not been allowed to visit Antana in hospital. Father told us those were the rules of the hospital — no children were allowed there. And we believed him. Now, I sometimes wonder whether the fare and the sheer physical impossibility of scrubbing us and finding clean and acceptable clothes for us to wear so that we would be decent enough not to disgrace the ailing nurse to her colleagues had anything to do with our never visiting Antana. Colored and white nurses worked at that hospital then. African nurses were a thing of the remote future. 1974 or thereabouts. Moreover, I think father, who worked at Chiappini Motors five minutes' walk from the hospital, would have found it very difficult to knock off work and then come for us in Retreat.

The funeral was a splendid affair. August. I had never seen such splendor in my home before that day. I have not since.

Nurses, beuniformed, in their hundreds, came to pay their last respects. African nurses. Colored and Indian nurses. White nurses. All in crisp, starched dresses, dresses so white it hurt your eyes to look at them. They had capes over their shoulders. Some navy and others red. All wore stiff white caps, in varying degrees of peakedness. This was the first time I saw buses at a funeral.

Mother had hastily returned; leaving her still-ailing father attended by relatives. She was inconsolable. It is my opinion that she has never completely recovered from this blow.

"Bampheka umtakaTata" ("They cooked father's child"), she says whenever the subject is brought up. It is not one we bring up often.

"They waited just until my back was turned, and then the filthy witches did their dirty deed. But, God is there," she comforts herself.

These are words said today, three decades after the sad event, said with a cold, white fury, a fury filled with the conviction of a God-ordained vengeance that mother knows awaits *"eliya gqwirha ngathi yingulube,"* that witch who is like a hog; awaits her with the certainty of the unerring heavens.

6

The year I left primary school was the year that education became racially segregated. Hitherto, white pupils, African pupils, colored pupils, and Indian pupils could, theoretically, attend the same school. Indeed, there were cases of African pupils attending colored or white schools. After 1955, the law forbade that practice. Henceforth there would be different Departments of Education for the different race groups. Understandably, the examinations set would not be the same since the examining bodies would be different.

Protesting against the Bantu Education Act of 1954, many African teachers were fired. Others were arrested. Some left the country, going to the newly independent African states, or to Britain. There were a few, I heard, who even went to Russia and elsewhere, countries I didn't even know existed.

Then, before I knew it, I was no longer a child. This seemed not to take everyone else the least bit by surprise. For me, however, when it finally came, it did so with alarming suddenness: one day I was envying the bigger girls their breasts; the next, I had sprouted these objects of my fervent desire.

"Sindiwe, tomorrow after school I want you to come to me at work."

My heart leapt. The next day was a Friday. We attached a great deal of importance to Friday in my family. That was the day on which father got paid. The first thing that came to my mind was "a dress!"

"No, you are not getting a dress. Your mother just made you one," replied Tata, to my disappointment.

Still optimistic nonetheless, I pestered him with guesses. But all he would say was, "If I told you what we'll be doing, you would have nothing to do with the information. So, wait and see. And besides," he added as an afterthought, "this way you can't go broadcasting it to your chums."

Not even Mama would satisfy the curiosity that dueled with excitement for first position. I knew well though, what I could count on: the five or so men who worked with Tata as petrol attendants were bound to give me some money. So would Tata, who never otherwise parted with a penny by giving it to his children.

That night as I ate my supper, stamped mealies, our staple food, I could already smell the fish and chips I would buy for myself with some of that money.

The hour or so I spent waiting for father to knock off from his job went without a hitch. I greeted his colleagues, who told me I had grown a lot since the last time I had come there. How I wanted to believe that! Grow, to me, meant added inches. That is something I didn't do well, and evidence thereof is my height today.

I had, as I had expected, been sent to the café to get cigarettes, matches, and cool drink.

"Take the change and buy yourself some sweets."

"Here," said another, "get yourself more."

Father worked the petrol pumps six to six. Thus a little after that hour, still without any illumination as to where we were going and why we were going there, I set off with him, mystified but uncomplaining.

A fifteen-minute walk took us from Observatory to Mowbray, where we took a bus. A short ride and a longish walk thereafter down a sandy footpath, guarded on either side by such thick hedge of maitland it could well have been a brick or concrete wall, and we were, of all places, on a livestock farm.

What was more astonishing, however, was that we were not there to visit a relative working there — the only conclusion I could reach after seeing our destination.

"This weekend," said my father, "we are going to celebrate your becoming a woman. Therefore, you are here to choose the little piece of meat we will offer our relatives, our friends, and our neighbors whom we have invited for these rites."

The farmer, like most farmers in this country, is white. Also, the probability is very high that he is an Afrikaner.

He called out to one of his African or colored men, *"Wat soek hy?"* ("What does he want?")

The man conveyed father's reply and instructed us, from his boss, to wait. The farmer was busy with someone else, a white man; customer, friend, or neighbor — I couldn't tell. He strode over to us as soon as he was free, with another of the servants in tow.

"Ask how much he can pay!" said the farmer in Afrikaans.

Father replied in English, directly to the farmer.

"Ask him whether he needs the delivery van," persisted the farmer, in Afrikaans, via his man.

After more of this "trialogue" we were eventually conducted to the stalls or stables. Here, as father had requested, we were shown the young heifers. Father asked me to pick out the one I liked best. I did.

"Thirty-five pounds," announced the farmer. Father replied he didn't think the heifer was worth that much as it was a bit on the thin side.

"Ask this body how much he has in his pocket. I haven't got the whole night to waste," roared the farmer, once more via his interpreter.

"No, *nkosi* (boss), I can pay twenty-five pounds."

"Take this one."

"That one is not right. It is too old."

After more haggling, we finally got the first heifer. Father paid twenty-seven pounds and ten shillings for it. We were leaving, halfway down the footpath, when the delivery van shot past us blowing a mini sandstorm in our way.

A hundred or so yards past, it lurched to a halt and one of the "boys" hollered:

"Niyayifun'ireyi?" ("Do you want a ride?")

Running forward, father indicated we did and urged me to hurry. I did.

Within three-quarters of an hour, the van came to a stop in front of my home. Father was the first to jump out and then helped me down, for there was no platform from the back of the truck. The two farmhands followed. They and father immediately started dragging the heifer out. The beast was secured by rope onto one of the poles supporting the wash line.

Father then went to the van's front compartment and thanked the farmer profusely for his kindness.

Seeds of ingratitude must have lurked somewhere inside me, even then. Father's profuse thanks irritated me.

Why was he thanking the boer for humiliating him? Father, my father, sharing the back of the van with a beast. I seethed, not at the farmer. Father should have refused the ride, I felt. I, for one, had no problems with the fare we would have paid had we made our own way. The time it would have taken us to get home, to say nothing of the inconvenience, were of little consequence to me. Fear of being kicked to a bloody pulp by the cow greatly added to my indignation. How dare this boer make us sit at the back? How dare he hog the front compartment, clearly roomy enough for three? Of course, I wasn't the least bit bothered by the two workmen's position. They could ride with a whole herd of cows as far as I was concerned. That was their job, after all.

By Sunday afternoon, the whole extended family seemed to have come. Men were seated outside in a circle in front of the house. Women filled the house. The younger were cooking. Some in the kitchen on the primus stoves — our two, and four others borrowed from neighbors. That food would be served to those deemed "elevated" — by age, wealth, or education, the usual criteria for such distinction.

Outside, a little beyond where the circle was emitting a collective cloud from the numerous pipes, a makeshift fireplace proudly displayed four-gallon cans, once containers of kerosene, wherein now bubbled meat, vegetables, and stamped mealies: a feast in the making.

Although everyone present knew the reason for the feast, at some point, before *umqombothi* (the home-brewed corn and *amabele* beer) went to the head, an announcement would be made:

"Will her mother or one of her aunts on her father's side, bring her out?"

Since father and I had returned from our little shopping, I had been in seclusion. Only mother or one of my father's own sisters were allowed near me. Now, mid-afternoon, I was summoned.

"Here she is!" Mother left me standing alone right there in the middle of the circle, now joined by the more mature women.

Uncle Masondo, the master of ceremonies, began a brief historical presentation. He had not quite finished when the bard of the clan deemed it fit to speed things up:

"Mzukulwana kaNophuthekezi,	"Grandchild of Nophuthekezi,
Ntombi kaSingongo, kaMbhuti	Daughter of Sigongo, of
	Mbhuti

KaMali, kaVongothwane!	Of Mali, of Vongothwane!
Mdengentonga!"	Tall by deeds!"
"Dlangamandla! Zulu! Tolo!	
Mchenge, Mabhanekazi	(The Praises of the Tolo Clan)
Vumba lempongo liyanuka!	
Mafungwashe kwezakwa-	(She by whom out of those of
Vongothwane!	Vongothwanes they swear!)
Thokazi leZizikazi	Heifer of a Zizi (Clan)
	woman
LamaZiz' amnyama neenkomo	(The Zizis, black as their
zawo!	cows!)
Camagu! Mpilo Nde! Amabutho	(Blessings, Long life! May
Akowenu akulondoloze!"	Your Ancestors guard you!)"

Ubulunga (the necklace woven from the tail hairs of the cow slaughtered for this rite) adorned my neck. Less ornate (and thus, to my mind, of less importance), were the belts I wore: one on my waist, two on each wrist, and a headband. All these came from different parts of the same "insignificant morsel." They would protect the woman for whom they had been made throughout her life but especially during her childbearing years.

I wore these bands for at least three months. Whenever I left the house, however, I wore only the waistband hidden well underneath, nestling against my skin.

If I had any doubt or sense of embarrassment about any of this, I wisely kept that to myself. Besides, the objective, to affirm, protect and enhance my womanhood, guaranteeing my fertility and safety during childbirth, was not something I was inclined to waive my rights to.

"My child, a good daughter pleases the parents. Your parents are very proud of you. Mind never to disgrace the Magona name. Mind never to disgrace the Tolo clan. Remember, a good wife is like a good daughter to her husband. She is also like a loving mother to him. We are all proud of you. Continue with school and learn so that when we are old we will have someone who can help us; someone to lean on."

"Dlangamandla, uzigcine ukhulile ngoku!" ("Dlangamandla, look after

yourself, you are grown now!") Those were the words from the women of my clan, said to me towards the end of the ceremony. I did not ask how I would protect myself. I did not ask where the danger lay. I was too busy feeling grown-up.

After the weekend celebrations I would go to school as usual. I had come to accept the existence of two far from compatible worlds, the one my world of traditions, rites, and ancestor worship, and the other, the world of "civilization" that included school. No word about what had happened to me would I whisper even to my most trusted friend once I was at school. By this time I was in high school.

The high school I had entered had been chosen unanimously. At that time, the Langa High School was the only high school for African students in the Western Cape. Students from as far away as Paarl, Stellenbosch, and Worcester commuted daily to this school. I was lucky to be living a mere twelve-mile distance from it.

That year, 1956, Langa High School must have had some of its youngest students entering high school. We would, during breaks, gaily play jump-rope and ball games, and run around screaming, laughing, and being thoroughly disgusting and undignified, according to some of the older students, who accused us of turning the school into a crèche. We were anywhere between twelve and fourteen.

I must have struck a rather pitiful-comic figure. Small, I was beuniformed in long gym-dress (father believed a woman, and to him that was any girl above the age of ten, should dress to cover not only the knee, but a good three to four inches below it).

"Shame, poor thing, why does your mother make you wear such a long gym-dress?" I was asked by two young married women, complete strangers, one day. That event led to the only conspiracy I remember between mother and me. Mother put in another set of buttons on the shoulder flaps of the gym. This permitted me to have two lengths — the first set of buttons were for father, giving me about three inches below the knee, and to be used on my way home, between Salt River and home where the likelihood of bumping into him existed. The second set gave me knee-length and teenaged respectability.

That same year I was attending confirmation classes. Every Saturday afternoon found me in a group inside the one-room shack we called church. There, the senior preacher, Mr. Ntenetye, quizzed us on the Catechism. Here, I fell hopelessly in love with the seductive melody of the Liturgy. When the day came, we went to St. George's Cathedral in Cape Town for confirmation by The Right Reverend Joost de Blank, the Archbishop of Cape Town. The whole ceremony had an air of unreality for me. If someone had told me I was already in Heaven, I would not have disputed that. Black, white, colored, and everybody else was there. All under one roof. And what a roof it was. Wherever did the saying "as poor as a church mouse" originate?

High-school students were more sophisticated. When they played truant, they went to the cinema, in Athlone, a predominantly colored and Muslim neighborhood, two miles away. Except for the films brought to the school by the Road Safety Council, or the Christian League, or another wholesome organization like that, I had not, till I was about to start teaching, been inside a movie house. I had only heard of titles like *The Robe, Zorro, The Girl Can't Help It, The Ten Commandments*, and others.

The most exciting film for me until age eighteen or nineteen, was *Samson and Delilah*, and I had seen it at school.

We were never shown any film relating to our school work; be it history, biology, English literature, or another subject. I was not to see the film *Jane Eyre*, prescribed reading for Form 3, till long thereafter. What combination of factors went into the making of this gross oversight, I cannot say.

Films are available in the city libraries. Was it custom? Or overwork? Or was it the policy of the government, always making the African feel unwelcome? I don't know.

I do know, however, that during my adulthood, we, the African sector of South Africa's populace, were forbidden the use of public libraries. Instead we were fobbed off with inadequate, silly, and insultingly inferior things: one-room structures furnished with whatever was being thrown out by royal whiteness; designated "our own"; and meant to satisfy accusers with statistical detail.

To those uninitiated to the double-talk that has been the insignia of the South African government, the worlds of difference between a library and a library would be hard to imagine. And that is precisely what the government banked on when its publications gave statistics on, for example, how many libraries (or hospitals, or schools, or housing units, or whatever) had been set aside for the exclusive use of each racial group.

I did one year of domestic science and changed to another subject the following year. Incredible though it may sound, it is the truth: in this urban environment, where a few students had electricity at home, we were being taught to use irons heated on the stove. The stove itself was a wood or coal burner. As far back as I can recall, mother has always had a Singer sewing-machine. Granted, a manually operated one, but a sewing-machine nonetheless. And here I was, learning to sew a garment using needle and thread. Talk about "keeping the native in her proper place"! White and even colored schools had modern appliances.

Similar contrasts existed in my home too. Jongi was bent on being a city boy. He did odd jobs to get pocket money. He sold newspapers on the street; collected bottles, rags, and bones and sold these to the rag man who came around every so often, hollering, *"been en bottel"* and perched on a mounting mound of bones and rags and bottles in the tired-horse-drawn cart.

With some of his money, Jongi often stole away and went to see films. We would call and call for him, and he would be nowhere to be found. This often happened on Saturday afternoons.

Father, determined to keep his children untarnished by the evils of the city and suspicious of all things modern, either figured out what was happening or was told by someone. Saturday evenings became duel nights: Father's beating strength pitted against Jongi's addiction. This went on for a long, long while until the night Jongi tried to avoid getting his retribution by pretending to be coal.

We had a *hokkie*, a little shed, adjacent to the house. Amongst the things we kept in it were bags of coal. It must have been winter, therefore. For we used coal for making fire in the brazier. Jongi found an empty sack, got inside, and held the open end as if it were tied in a knot.

Father, perhaps getting anxious about the safety of his eldest child, a son, as the evening went on and Jongi failed to make an appearance, began leaving the house, a little too nonchalantly, only to return asking,

67

"This boy isn't here yet?"

I have never found out what made him suspect the *hokkie*. And, having suspected it, the bags. However, father went out and apparently secured the "knot" and began beating the "coal." "You'll kill him! You'll kill him! Tolo, leave my child alone, do you hear me?" Mama, looking and sounding like one demented, finally managed to rescue "her" child. A very blackened sorry-looking hopefully-bioscope-saturated lad was ushered into the house.

However, some good came of this episode: Jongi could go, one Saturday per month, to see a film *if* all his chores were done *and* his school work didn't suffer *and* he went to church the next morning. To me, this was less an example of the magnanimity of my loving parents than it was, yet again, a sign of how everyone favored Jongi. I wasn't even allowed to join the Girl Guides. And all because I was a girl.

But then again, I had to admit, Jongi had paid dearly for the freedom he won.

7

I doubt that my high-school teachers saw me as anything but the imbecile I couldn't help being, in stark contrast to my primary-school days. My primary-school teacher would have been amazed at the transformation. The model pupil of only yesterday was no more: the one who had courted their approval, even risking the ire of her mates, had, in high school, become a teachers' pest. Once, when I was still at primary school, we had been given a new poem and told to learn one verse overnight. I had memorized the whole thing from "I wandered lonely as a cloud" to "And dances with the daffodils!" — putting to shame most of my classmates.

The thrashing they got was doubled.

"If Cynthia could do so much, what is your excuse?" had thundered the teacher with each "tywa-aa-ash!" of the switch.

That little episode earned me a terrible name among my classmates although I could never, for the life of me, figure out what I had done wrong.

Where I had distinguished myself at primary school as a bright student, one of six out of a class of eighteen to pass the external examinations for Standard Six, my high-school career was an unmitigated failure.

I found high school bewilderingly unstructured through, perhaps, having been too structured. Where I had, until then, had a teacher, one teacher, for the whole year, I now had a teacher per subject. And although I had a class teacher, that didn't seem to have much to do with anything. Occasionally, the class teacher would make a façade of keeping a register of attendance. But, I came to feel, nobody really knew me. Not in the same way as teachers at my primary school.

I floundered through the first two years and scraped into Form 3 or Junior Certificate. Besides making the first team in netball, nothing noteworthy happened to me. Unless seemingly uncontrollable misdemeanors count. Any time my name was mentioned at assembly or I was asked to step out, it was for admonishment.

"Magona, you are a boredom in the school!" and all eyes turn to me for, although Jongi had been a student in this school two years prior to my arrival, everyone knew to which "Magona" the principal was referring.

Strange how Jongi somehow managed to be well behaved at school! Not that I killed anybody either. My sins were such petty things as talking or laughing or playing in class. All rather innocent really. "Rowdy behavior," it was labeled, taken seriously, and gave me a bad name.

One of my greatest weaknesses was laughter. Uncontrollable laughter coupled with a mind too slow to erase a picture and render itself blank. A typical scenario would be as follows:

The teacher is out of the classroom. A buffoon does something very very funny. Everyone laughs. The teacher steps in. All smiles disappear and all laughter stops. Just like that? The faces that have been crinkled and contorted in abandonment barely a second ago are now perfect pictures of studiousness. That used to kill me!

I would laugh and laugh and laugh until the tears rolled down my cheeks, the quizzical look on the teacher's face a spur rather than a deterrent. In my mind I retained the faces of a minute ago which, contrasted to the ones I was looking at, produced such incongruity.

Little wonder, therefore, that I was far from popular in high school.

Not only did I tend to be silly (one teacher once had me write five hundred lines of "I am a frivolous little fool unfortunately not blessed with sense or composure"), I was younger than most of my classmates. Moreover, being Jongi's sister was a clear disadvantage in this respect. All the boys, scared of him, gave me a very wide berth indeed.

Shunned by most students, disliked by my teachers, I was not however completely bereft of friends. I was a very active member of the school's IDC (I Don't Care) Group, the jolly group of students every school knows too well; the students who, on the fringe of all sanctioned school business, are right in the thick of things forbidden.

By Form 3, I had become so adept at covering my tracks I could sleep right through a forty-five-minute tedious history class on the Phoenicians, or another equally fascinating aspect of antiquity, without a single nod. The lessons were delivered in droning unrelieved monotone: a pair of sunglasses and an air of mystified stupor were the only allies I needed.

Needless to say, such ingenuity assured me a fail at the end of the year.

8

1958 was a bad year to fail. Three years earlier, African education had entered a new phase. Not only was it legally segregated, but the new department perceived its syllabus as so superior that anyone joining the Bantu Education stream midway was forced to go back a year.

The 1959 Form Threes had been in Bantu Education since 1956. Those of us who had failed, supposedly wouldn't be able to cope. We had to go back to Form Two. Repeating Form Three would have been bad enough as it would mean that the three-year course would take me four years. But this new rule meant that it would be five years before I obtained my Junior Certificate. I would be gray-haired by then. Belatedly, I saw the folly of my ways.

After tearful beseechings on my part, my parents agreed to send me to boarding school.

Again, the choice of school was determined by the exigencies of the case. Any school good enough to turn a blind eye to the "back one year" rule was a godsend.

Reliable location telegraph had it that Lourdes Secondary School in uMzimkhulu was such a school.

I applied. I got in.

Another of the peculiarities of black education is, and has been, the unfailing delays in releasing the results of external examinations. Although I should have known without being told, it was not until late January, after schools had reopened, that I learnt of my failure.

Therefore, by the time I had persuaded my parents I was worth the sacrifice, that they should waste more money on someone as undeserving as me, it was mid-February. They now had to borrow the money. The whole process — application, funding, and acceptance— took care of another month.

I eventually started school at the beginning of the second term, in April.

In the "must bring" list, were articles such as nighties and sheets. These were things my family never bought (the ones the grown-ups used came to our house via relatives working as domestic servants in private homes, hospitals, or hotels). Now, a pair of sheets and two nightdresses were bought (not made) for me!

Everything I took with me was packed into a 2 x 1 x 2 crudely made wooden suitcase.

UMzimkhulu is perhaps less than five hours' drive from where I was born. Lourdes was a Catholic institution. My memory may be playing tricks on me, but I seem to recall that the day in this institution did not begin at crack of dawn. It began before: at four o'clock, to be precise.

Silence, until after morning prayers. Then breakfast. More prayer; followed by morning classes, at seven o'clock. Regular school began at eight-thirty and ended at three. The day was broken at midday for the Angelus: more prayer. And, thank God: lunch. We had dinner at five, went to the Grotto (for more prayer) at six. The nuns were quietly insistent and definitely successful in keeping us in line.

At Lourdes, as had happened to me before, I was fascinated by the sound, meaning (when I understood), and color of the Liturgy. Also, my Latin improved tremendously, thanks to the Mass (said in Latin). Philanthropy took root: singing a hymn that I think began,

71

"Oh Lady of Fatima, Hail," we, for some reason, sang the line "lead Russia back home again" very loudly. No doubt, we were expressing the instinctive urge of all human beings to save any in need of such saving. No one ever took the trouble to tell me, though, exactly what danger menaced this land. But then, who stops to ask if the fire in a neighbor's house was started by the primus stove exploding or the children playing with matches? Not me.

The simplicity, rigid orderliness, and terrible diet, as well as wounded pride, helped me focus on my studies. Smaller classes were a boon: a golden opportunity for me to attract attention to myself in profitable, wholesome ways.

Moreover, Bantu Education, even after only a few years of existence, was already bearing its bitter fruit. Those students who were from the old stream were faring much, much better than the products of this exclusively African system.

We of "the old school" felt not a little superior.

The nine months I spent at Lourdes were easily the most productive of my entire high-school career. At the end of the year, I was richly rewarded by passing even the subjects I had started only that year: math, social studies, and Afrikaans. And, I think I became a little more human too.

St. Matthew's Teacher Training College was my next port of call. Having completed three years of high school, I was to begin training as a primary-school teacher. At that time, such a course still existed; for Africans only.

By now there were six children in our family. Money was tight; but I didn't realize how tight till much later.

Although I had decided, during the summer holidays, that at this school I would learn a game such as tennis, as befits a teacher, this was not to be. My prowess at netball preceded me to St. Matthew's and I was forced, in ever so nice a manner, to be in the netball team. Flattered, I consoled myself I would do as I pleased the following year, when I would not be a newcomer. Only, my second and last year of training saw me leading the team as its captain.

The subjects taught at the training college were far from strenuous. The load, though, was very heavy. And on top of that, there were practicals — sewing, knitting, practice teaching. Learning to

72

make teaching aids — collages, maps, charts, lists — when even drawing stick figures made me break out in cold sweat, was no picnic. But, there were ways around obnoxious courses: doing another's ironing or laundry was considerably preferable; a fair exchange.

I studied well and enjoyed most of the work. Rumbustiousness would have been a fault, but disarming honesty redeemed.

"Oh the good old duke of York!
He had ten thousand men.
He marched them up to the top of the hill
And he marched them down again."

This is an example of the kind of innocent mischief I was prone to. Instead of ending the first line with "York" I had yelled "Kent." Quite by coincidence, one of the teachers happened to be passing our little parade. He was far from amused. Just as, as a sign of respect, children did not say adults' names, students did not say teachers' names. *Ukuhlonipha*, the custom forbidding married women to say any names of their husband's elders or even words with syllables similar to these, had become part of the code of conduct of schools.

Mr. Kente, the senior Xhosa teacher, summoned us into the biggest of the classrooms. He reminded us, in no uncertain terms, of the money our poor parents were paying to have us in that school; of our duty to those self-denying parents; of the real danger of expulsion for gross misconduct, then pounced:

"Which one of you shouted 'Kent'?"

Silence. Deafening silence.

"All right then," said the fuming teacher, "stand in line," bracing himself to deal with us all.

Whilst I understood the solidarity thus expressed when a lot of girls knew the culprit, I couldn't remain silent and let others suffer — especially since that would not save my skin either!

So, stepping out of the group I acknowledged my guilt.

Mr. Kente must have been mighty relieved. Thrashing 200 girls can be a sweaty, exhausting job. He would have punished himself more than us.

He forgave me.

9

The first year was soon over. This meant that I had one more year of formal education before I joined the ranks of working people — teachers, to be precise.

That summer, during the December-January school holidays, I realized that that would be the last summer holiday I would have as a student. Petrified, I faced the fact that I was far from ready to be a serious adult.

Calmly, I took stock of my personal inventory, the characteristics I would be bringing to the profession, come end of the coming year. I had to come to the conclusion a drastic image overhaul was indicated.

When I went back to school, the newcomers, beginning their training that year and not hindered by their knowledge of me the previous year, could not believe I had been friends, very close friends, with another student, who, because she had failed first year, was in their class.

Dorothy hadn't changed noticeably during the summer: completely unhampered by the weight, so heavy on my own shoulders, of the imminence of the duty of educator, shaper of character and of destinies: where I had assumed such an air of grownupness, ladylike in appearance, voice, step, and deed, Dorothy was as exuberant and loud as we had been the previous year. Her spontaneous and highly audible raucous laughter, our trademark of yesterday, the random and rowdy galloping that had passed for walking briskly then, as well as the appearance, without fail, of her name on the list of offenders, read out Saturdays, were in stark contrast to my newfound sedateness.

So unbelievable was the fact of our ever having had anything in common that, once, some of the newcomers actually came to me and in hushed tone asked:

"Sisi, is it true that you and Dorothy were friends last year?"

If I had had any doubt about my decision to see less of Dorothy, the respect I detected in the reverence-filled voices as well as the fact of being addressed as "sisi," assured me I had done what I ought to do; it was the right thing, though it worried me.

Oh, Dorothy and I would, if we happened to bump into each other, have a brief chat. However, just as students also exchanged pleasantries with the kitchen staff but were well aware of the yawning cleavage between what kitchen staff was doing and what they would soon be doing, so did I try to remember the irreconcilable differences between the two of us. I was mature and ready to face the world of professionals and Dorothy could not be accused of any such.

Thus did the hapless Dorothy become a casualty of my rebirth and my zeal. That she was repeating first year just made it easier to execute the plan I had formulated during the summer holiday: not seeing her during the school day made it possible for me to overlook the balance sheet where the gains, if such they were, definitely did not warrant such capital outlay.

There were frequent lapses, however. Dorothy and I had lengthy heart-to-heart sessions, jaunts to the nearby bushes to pick *isipingo* berries or, and more often, study sessions when she thought I could help her with some aspect of her work.

Of course, I did not realize my loss until years later. I was too busy basking in my self-importance. Mrs. Maarman, the boarding school mistress, announced at one of the Saturday morning assemblies, "How I wish every student could be like Cynthia Magona!" The offenses were particularly large in number and of more serious and disturbing nature than the usual prank; talking during silence of study periods, or untidiness. And I, saint-like, had none.

My transformation led to my being a prefect in all but name. I was asked to perform the duties of prefects; box inspection, studies monitoring, outings supervision; and on me fell the most desirable chore, the plum: I had the honor of fetching Mrs. Maarman's pail of hot water in the morning. As this meant I went to the kitchen, filled the pail to the brim, poured a quarter of the water into mine waiting on the way, I was the envy of every girl in the bathroom. As we stood, bent over pails of icy water or washed directly under the tap, mine was at least tepid. For, after adding enough cold water to have enough to share with closest friends, it could not but be tepid.

1961 June holidays.

Tall, well-built, strikingly good-looking — even all this would not do justice to the man I met one day during my last winter vacation as a student.

He came, a vision, striding lazily towards the bus stop where I patiently awaited the appearance of a bus. He was going to see a film. I was going to Cape Town station to buy my ticket and make reservations for the journey back to school. We sat next to each other on that bus ride!

By the time he got off, about half an hour later, I was no longer in doubt about my femininity or desirability.

Poised at the threshold of the world of work, professional work, a teaching career, I was advised by a family friend to go on and complete high school. Six months before completion of the two-year training course, when I was already sending out applications for a position, this was advice I certainly wasn't going to listen to. How could she have known that she was talking to someone who saw herself highly qualified and ready to assume the responsibilities of a schoolteacher, a role whose weight I already felt? The attentions of an attractive man would have expelled any lingering doubts about my readiness to enter adulthood; mine melted away so fast, I forgot I'd had any.

That last week of vacation went so fast; what with answering his daily letters, going to the movies with him (his passion, my initiation to such heady pastimes).

We continued corresponding after I had returned to school. And I was told how I was missed in every letter I received. Bliss was my middle name! Like good rains after a long hard-hitting drought, his attention and his words healed a wound I had nursed all my life. Once, my dear father, not realizing he was dealing me a mortal blow, had told me this story:

"When you were born, I took one look at you and fled to cry behind the hut."

That is how ugly I had been. Poor father!

He had meant well by telling me the story, for to him there was a happy ending: his grandmother, Nophuthekezi, finding him thus stricken, had chided him: "You, ungrateful thing! It is not enough God has blessed you with a healthy daughter. NO! You cry because there isn't a blade on her head! Oh, how silly you are! Yes! And how blind!"

"After those words, she had left me there wondering how on earth I could have been that stupid. Okay! So you had less hair than an egg and you were so black, with lips — unbelievable! — even blacker! And I had been thinking to myself, 'Dear God, and she is a girl! Who will ever marry her?' But she made me see I was mindless."

After that, father had returned to the hut, picked me up into his arms and, according to him, "fell incurably in love with" me. "Ooh," he had gone on, expansively, "anyone who dares tell you now your hair is short doesn't know what she or he is talking about!" Poor father! All he succeeded in doing, trying to show me how much my looks had improved, was confirm in me how hopeless my situation was. Who has ever heard of any ugly baby?

It didn't help that others outside my immediate family shared my opinion. Everyone who, on meeting me for the first time heard I was Jongi's sister, predictably responded, "Yes, you look alike." Pause. "But he is soo-o handsome!"

In this respect, even my mental ability caused me pain. Two goddesses, big girls who were high-school students, attending boarding school away from Cape Town, had asked me to plait their hair. They must have been preparing to go back to school for they wanted one of the more intricate styles. I was doing my best and they were unstinting in their praise. They even gave me some money and some chocolate. It was while I was still aglow at being the subject of their kindness that one of them said, "She is soo-o good!" To which the other responded: "Yes, but Y-L-G-U!"

I went on looking happy, plaiting hair. I was too hurt to show it and too scared to let them know I knew what they had said about me. After all, it wasn't their fault I, at age seven or eight, could spell backwards. I recognized their attempt to protect me.

Anyone with that kind of brutally clear picture of her plainness would have been stark mad not to approach adolescence with an enormous inferiority complex. No one had accused me of insanity. And now I had the most handsome man on earth telling me I was beautiful. And, I knew he meant it too.

Reluctantly, my parents accepted this new aspect of my life. Luthando was allowed to come into the house to see me. If we were going out, he didn't have to rely on the customary whistling or other sign to let me know he was waiting for me outside. He could send a child to tell me he was there or he could come in.

I think rather than their being overjoyed at this development, my parents thought letting him in was more in keeping with my status — I would be teaching soon. The only thing that marred what would have been my overflowing cup was the absence of enthusiasm from Jongi. He was polite to Luthando, too polite for my peace of mind. But that was not anything on which my mind dwelt long: I was too busy being happy.

10

The last school report, September of the final year of my training, is filled with teachers' comments where, I swear, teachers seem to vie with each other regarding the praises they could shower on me:

"It is a joy to teach Cynthia!" — a comment I liked so much that many are the times I have used it in the case of a particularly deserving student.

And: "Such a diligent student should be congratulated on an excellent examinations result!"

Another, "Cynthia has qualities that will undoubtedly serve her well in the future."

And yet another, "Good luck to an industrious student!"

It would have taken a much stronger personality than mine not to end up with a swollen head.

A perfect school year had been marred by three events which, seemingly unrelated, have come to form a trilogy, stubbornly linked in my own mind: I was forced to apply for the reference book; there was an accident and two students died; South Africa became a Republic.

1961 was my eighteenth year. From age sixteen, every African was obliged to carry a pass on his or her person at all times on pain of arrest. I had managed to postpone this by remaining at school, though even that was breaking the law. Now that I was leaving school, I complied. Not doing so would have complicated things later and caused a great deal of trouble.

The college still used the pit lavatory system. Sewage is thus not removed but lies rotting in pits six feet deep. The pits are covered with wood floors on which stand rows of seats. At St. Matthew's, the cubicles, facing each other, had no doors.

Girls would go to these toilets running, although we were constantly warned against this practice. But we were warned not to do so many things that I doubt any of us took this particular warning any more seriously than the others.

One day the floor gave way and two of the student-teachers plunged into the pit and drowned.

South Africa held a referendum in 1961 to decide whether or not the country should continue its ties with Great Britain and remain within the Commonwealth. The English element of the white South African populace favored keeping this "connection" whilst the Afrikaner element was for breaking ties with England. No one saw any need to consult people of color.

The Afrikaner won the day; South Africa became a republic.

Yes, these three events are not really linked. But, perhaps because it is through them that I caught the first glimpse of my own impuissance, in my memory they are firmly twined; strands of the same hideous whole. In them, terribly articulated, was our voicelessness, meticulously designed by the powers that be; our forever being blamed for the untenable condition others have imposed on us; and the squandering, the systematic extinguishing of the breath of a people by rank bigotry and evil incarnate.

Shortly after the republic was announced, a spontaneous one-day strike erupted at the school. There were complaints about the food; about suspension from class when fees were not paid on time; and about teacher shortage.

"Cynthia must have instigated this," said the powers that be. "She is a natural leader," they added, confirming their own suspicions.

I had been surprised by the action and, to this day, I believe the whole thing was spontaneous.

I marveled and was saddened and hurt at how my erstwhile virtues were now used to discredit me.

As the end drew near, farewell functions became the order of the day. Words of wisdom flowed freely. Among some of the more memorable advice is — "Girls, when you see the broken, dirt-filled nails of your mothers' hands; when you see the gnarled fingers and cracked palms; don't ever feel ashamed of them. Remember, your mothers tilled the soil with their bare hands; they harvested the farmers' crops so that you would never have to do the same." This came from the wife of the principal, herself an excellent teacher and compassionate disciplinarian.

The principal and his wife were English. They had come to South Africa shortly after their marriage. For decades, they had "served" the African: teaching had been their life and they had taught in this teacher-training school and taught well. They were on the brink of retirement. Like so many well-intentioned white people, ministers of religion, teachers, doctors, nurses, politicians, housewives, and others, they were in South Africa to do something for the natives. This was a three-hundred-year-long project that seemed nowhere near completion, judging from statements issuing from government officials: "One should not compare our bantus with the American negro, who is much more developed."

Then, as now, I was baffled as to how people who had been slaves could have outdistanced those never so blighted. How is it that after so many people of goodwill left their own shores, forsaking family and the familiar, relinquishing title and wealth, spurred by noble desire to serve and uplift, sparing not their strength nor their soul; wave upon wave of selfless humanitarians; how is it that after all that, descendants of these same agents of good can say with no sense of failure, "They are not yet ready" about those they had all sought to elevate?

I have yet to hear evaluation blaming the teacher, his motives, or his methods.

11

Thus armed with an inordinately inflated sense of my own importance based on what turned out to be a hopelessly inadequate preparation for the work I was embarking on, and with little understanding of the forces at play, I set forth.

With next to no idea of what was in store for me, no idea of the gaping schism between the simulated classes, including practice teaching, and the horrible heavy reality of a class made up of an unchanging group of little people who, with their optimistic parents, expect to be changed, progressively and cumulatively, for their betterment, expect this without knowing that they expect a miracle with a capital M, I began teaching.

It wasn't long before I realized that all the things I had learnt when supposedly undergoing training were a sham, a cruel mockery, a hollow promise. I was demoralized.

Lack of books is endemic in African schools. More than half the pupils in the first class I taught did not have books. This not-havingness occurred in numerous variations. Some would have some of the textbooks and none of the exercise books. Others would have a few of the textbooks and almost all of the exercise books. There were those who had very few of either and those who had none at all. Some had all the exercise books and not one textbook; whilst there were a few with all the textbooks and only one or two exercise books. One girl had all the books. She even had a pen, a pencil, a ruler, an eraser, and a handkerchief.

Needless to say, interesting though such configurations are, they wreak havoc with the teacher's well-laid plans. Furthermore, those pupils who had any of the required books were in daily danger of losing them to those who didn't and knew they would not be buying them the next day, or the next, or the next.

Not having books is one of the misdemeanors punishable by corporal punishment. The beatings and probably the sheer embarrassment that must surely accompany the daily proclamation of one's poverty, prompted a lot of the pupils to pilfer. The very young do not always understand that poverty is supposed to be ennobling . . .

We preached the parable of Heaven's inaccessibility to the wealthy, the eye of the needle story. We taught these poor children how to be poor. All the Child Psychology, all the Principles of Education, all the Method of Teaching, all the School Organization I had learnt during my training, just didn't figure, didn't make any sense at all. It had not and never would be meant for these children.

I had not been trained to teach children from poor homes; a decided flaw when one realizes that probably only ONE per cent, if that, of the African population group does not earn depressed wages. I had been trained to teach children from homes where there was a father and a mother. I had been trained to teach children of working parents. The children in my class came mostly from women-headed homes. And those women stayed in at their places of employment: they were busy being smiling servants minding white babies. These children came from homes where, although parents worked, there was no money.

In this respect, the good fortune of a happy childhood did nothing to supplement the deficiency of my professional training: my own sheltered childhood, including adolescence, an idyllic interlude, had left me an innocent. I thought I knew so much of my world; yet I was almost unaware of the injustices.

In severing the education of the African child from that of the white child, the powers that be had announced, in Parliament, that the aim was to ensure that the black child would be protected from frustration; she would not be put through an education that would make her believe she was being prepared to graze the greener pastures. The education that would be given to the African child, the Honorable Dr. Verwoerd had enlightened us, would fit her for her station in life, service to her master, the white man, woman, child, and, in permissible ways, the white economy. Service, not participation, never mind access, would be the operative, the key word.

There had been no scarcity of pointers to my destiny. But is anyone as blind as she who will not see? Or as deaf as she who will not hear?

Lessons were about to start, for me!

The world goes awry

I have never been rich and the chances that I will ever be thus burdened are almost nonexistent. However, like so many of my generation — children of parents poor, loving, caring, and God-fearing — I had not known I was poor. Oh, sure, I knew we didn't have furniture, we didn't have a car, we didn't have shoes or fine clothes, and meat was a rare sighting. But none of the children with whom I was growing up were any better. In fact, a lot were worse off.

Dessert is a dish I still associate with Father Ramsey, God rest his soul, the itinerant English priest who came to our parish on what appeared, to me as a child, as infrequently as Christmas but what probably was a quarterly basis. On some of these occasions, the good man of God would also visit some of the parish families. I think it would be a safe bet to say though his visits, to our home particularly, are etched indelibly in my mind, he probably stopped at our house no more than five or six times all told. Those were the times we had custard and jelly.

Yes, food for me has always been a necessity, sustenance for the body. The idea of ice cream or any food for pleasure, is as foreign to me as a silk dress would be to a peasant maiden.

However, I had done what was supposed to ease my lot and elevate me a little beyond the grinding poverty that is the status of the African in South Africa. I expected to earn more, to be precise; the rest would accrue therefrom, I reasoned.

In the history of my family, going back three or four generations, except for one of father's uncles, a forester, I was breaking virgin ground. Although Jongi had passed his Junior Certificate before me and was now grappling with matric, I had not only passed JC, I had a professional certificate: I was a qualified teacher.

The year was 1962. I was leaving my teens behind me, entering the world of work, unfamiliar terrain. A year before, we, my own family and all other African families, had been moved from Retreat to Nyanga West, later renamed Guguletu. A massive dislocation, the result of the government's slum-clearance drive.

Nyanga West added to the sense of disjointedness, the all-embracing unreality I found myself immersed in. I was going through many changes at a giddier pace than I had been prepared for. I left school at the same time that I plunged into womanhood and took a lover. In Nyanga West, I found myself in the midst of a conglomeration, rather large in number, of ill-assorted people, strangers brought together by the zeal of the government to control our lives.

I had grown up knowing almost everybody in the community, the little community of Retreat. That well-knit, lawful community had been scattered, willy-nilly, like grains of sand during a whirlwind. Nearly three decades following this enforced exodus, there are friends I have not seen since. Some I've bumped into, rarely and years ago. I have been blessed with the continuous friendship of lamentably very few others.

"Spoilers." A new word entered my vocabulary. A chilling word. A word conjuring pirate-like characters became part of my living in Guguletu. Spoilers. Fearless and feared, a law unto themselves. Thugs who preyed on straggling individuals, newly-transplanted from Retreat, from Kensington and from Athlone, from Simonstown, from Addersvlei, from Cape Town itself, and from everywhere else Africans had called home.

84

The windswept, treeless miles-from-anywhere township, they were told, was their home. Our Pride, Guguletu, the powers that be would have the gall to baptize it, openly declaring to all skeptics their unwavering pursuit: the destruction of African family life, communal life, and all those factors that go toward the knitting of the very fabric of a people. In the nearly three decades I've lived in Guguletu, I have never seen one squirrel there. And I've often wondered why.

I spent that summer, my first in Nyanga West, my first as a full-fledged, about-to-work grown-up, filled with a sense of my own importance. Certainly, this seemed to be validated by how important I was to Jongi, whose brotherly solicitude knew no bounds; to Luthando who paid me heady attention and made me believe he had been waiting for me, all his life; to my parents, whose prayers, I knew, had been answered: was I not visible, living proof that hard work, their hard work, had paid off? As some people measure success with models of cars, real estate, vacations, bonds and other savings, Africans point to their (hopefully) educated offspring and say, out loud:

"I may have nothing to show for my years of toil, but I have educated (*Ndifundisile*)"; that is, put a child through school.

Yes, all these people made me know, in their different ways, that I was a person of worth. Why? Even neighbors congratulated my mother, and my father, on their extreme good fortune: that, "In these children of today, children who break every law of their parents, you have been blessed with a daughter who listened to you and went on to finish her education."

Jongi was a clerk at the Administration office. Then, Nyanga West had one such office. Later, there would be three; and this first would come to be known as the Section 1 administration office of *Kwa-Rhosini* (at Goosen's). Goosen was the name of the white Superintendent there. No senior officials of the Bantu Administration were ever black.

New in Guguletu (I had only been there during the June holidays), I found Jongi's protectiveness particularly handy and reassuring. He would walk me to the shops at Nyanga. He would accompany me to the bus stop or train station if I were going out of Nyanga West.

The first sign that all was far from well came when no teaching job was thrust in my lap as schools re-opened. The first quarter of school progressed and I was doing something I had longed for for years: twiddling my thumbs. Only, this occupation was far from the bliss I had believed it to be.

Father began hinting at what might be at the root of my problem: I had omitted to offer the Secretary of the School Board "something" and people were telling him it would be donkey's years before I would get a post if we did not oil this gentleman's palm.

My professional foot went firmly down. Why would I, highly educated, allow myself to be led backward? If I yielded to the suggestion of bribery, I would be a stone's throw away from the witchdoctor's cleansing incisions, if not much worse. Now, I chose to remember and bear witness to the motto of the Langa High School, "Let Your Light So Shine!"

Fortunately, no sooner did I begin a frantic search for a job, any job, than I was employed at what was then the only fisheries in Guguletu.

I was to work there for two full months; frying fish, selling fish, gorging myself on fish crumbs, working from eight in the morning till midnight; twenty rand a month with deductions for shortages.

I learnt fear. No, I was no stranger to fear. But, until the spoilers of Nyanga West became a reality in my life, I had not known pervasive fear, groundless, free-floating, unconnected. Until then, my fear had been rooted in a deed, my deed. My wrong deed. In my book, only such an act, performed by me, could provoke fury in another. Therefore, I had need or cause to fear. But only if I had wronged another. I wore my purity like a shield, sure in the knowledge of my safety. Mindful, to wrong none.

Never had it occurred to me that a complete stranger could wish me dead — no, could cause my death, kill me. Deliberately. And for no reason, no wrong on my part. He would only want me dead.

This knowledge threw every assumption I had about sane people away. Mad people, I knew, could kill. But then, their minds were twisted. Their thoughts, scrambled. Their worldview upside down. My world threw me back into myself. Into the core that only I can enter. Where not even lovers can penetrate. Only dread.

Spoilers were not only not mad, they were actually smarter than the average person, weren't they? If they could get away with so much, escape the wrath of such a punitive government, to say nothing of township-dwellers, surely, they were smarter. I was beginning to learn of our utter impotence. The adults I had grown up seeing as powerful, were being blown helter-skelter, and showing me they were ill-equipped to fly in the face of man-made storms.

I had known of the pass before coming to Nyanga West; but a pass raid was new to me. I understood liquor raids, which could include pass raids. But, for the police to go out, in full force, with no other objective than to arrest people whose passes were "wrong" or who had forgotten their passes at home, was something I had not been exposed to.

Police presence in the township had absolutely no correspondence to the committing of criminal acts. The spoilers freely roamed the streets of Nyanga West, molesting maidens, beating up youths despised for looking decent, breaking and entering people's houses, raping, killing, and tramping on every known moral code, banking on the very law-abidingness of their victims.

The blessing of a loving brother doubled, linked to my very survival. Father, and all men his age, commanded less respect among this pack of wild animal-like youth than did Jongi. The spoilers saw in the older generation, *iimurhu*, unsophisticated village yokels ripe for plucking. The common decency and moral uprightness of people of my parents' generation became a label or synonym for dotage or borderline idiocy, in the keen eyes of *oomanwaza*. The razor-sharp, streetwise youth who prided themselves on their worldly ways, pitied, scorned, and derided "common" people who lived to work, actually put themselves through this daily ritual, this torture, just to earn money. They had found an easier way of becoming monied. They simply took it from those stupid enough to sweat for it. Kill them, if they made that unpleasant, soiling affair necessary. Killing smelled of hard work. Spoilers would rather not be put to all that trouble. So it was said, they appreciated "customers" or "birds" who didn't resist plucking.

My carefree days were over. Always a coward, the fear that was thus taught me was never ever to leave me. I, who had never looked at the eyes of a murderer, began seeing a murderer in every pair of unknown eyes.

Mornings, Jongi walked me to the shops. To do this, he would walk a little past his job. We both started work at eight o'clock. So we made it a point to leave a little earlier than we would have done, so we could walk togther without rushing and without either one of us being late.

Once I was in the shop, I was on my own. The other workers, aware that I was a "lady teacher," often teased me: "How come you're sweating here with us when you're educated?" However, it was done in a spirit of camaraderie and I responded accordingly. Frankly, it had not occurred to me I would not be in school, teaching, come opening day. And, even after that came to pass, I remained optimistic I'd soon be teaching. Unemployment, not the concept but the very word, was unknown to me. Once, a long time ago, father had been out of work. In the nature of childhood hardships, this event had made not a dent in my world view. And, after all, hadn't I been schooled into the firm belief that education virtually assured one of lifelong job security. Why, then, would I have been worrying?

Soon, however, the days began to feel long. Standing, day long, from morn till dusk and beyond, had a rather dampening effect on my enthusiasm. I began to chafe. My ankles took to swelling. The fresh fried fish I had looked forward to became less and less appetizing. Besides, the smell clogged my very pores, perfumed my hair, and, even after airing, washing, ironing, and airing (again), my clothes would still smell of fish.

Then the gods smiled on me. During the March–April 10-day school vacation, I was called into the offices of the School Board and there given a contract. At the beginning of the second quarter, in April, my dream would come true. I would be a Standard Three teacher at the Hlengisa Higher Primary School in Nyanga.

A desperate secret became mine. Throughout the two years of teacher-training I had undergone, not once had I heard mention of teachers' salaries. As an entrance level teacher, I would earn, per month, eleven pounds nineteen shillings and eleven pence. AmaXhosa say, *"Kukho ipeni engekhoyo"* ("There is a penny short") to indicate mental illness or craziness. I still do not know the significance of the missing penny from African teachers' salaries.

2

I began teaching after the Easter holidays. Not too soon, either. In the short time of being an employee at the fisheries, my great love of fish had completely evaporated. Its slimy, smelly, and oily (when cooked) nature was only part of the cause of my reaction. The cruder side of business peeled my eyelids — the suspicion employers hold of their workers, their violent aversion to loss, that all too often leads to the abuse, exploitation, and even beatings of the workers. The employer was a black man.

Dressed in a beige terylene skirt with soft gray and light brown stripes, a blouse I can no longer remember, and a dark gray cardigan with collar, two front pockets, and brass buttons, almost a blazer, and beige kid gloves, I felt every inch a teacher as I walked to Nyanga East that morning, to start on my new job. Darling Jongi walked me all the way to the corner of NY 78 and NY 3 right where the latter changes to Sithandathu Avenue, marking the border between Nyanga East and Nyanga West.

I was to trudge this long road many more days, and feel the anguish of feet trapped in ill-fitting shoes, feet trapped in nylon stockings on days far from cool, feet, step by painful step, walking the long distance there and back. There was no bus service between the two Nyangas. No one I knew had a car. My father who worked hard all his life, died, a decade later, still carless. In fact, he died without even a bicycle. And he had worked his life away in a garage.

Young, idealistic, and inexperienced, I have seventy-two pupils in my class. If all had been well, each would be between eleven and twelve years old. Standard Three, the class I teach, is their fifth year of school.

However, all is not well. The pupils range, in age, from nine to nineteen years. The real bewildering discrepancy, however, is in the skills they demonstrate — be it in math, language or general knowledge, in personal hygiene or sense of responsibility.

When I discovered pupils who could not perform elementary arithmetic operations such as adding five and two, I resorted to methods more in line with beginners: drawing circles on the floor and "adding" stones, in a vain attempt at remedial teaching. The fact that I knew dangerously little about that did not hinder me. I didn't know what else to do.

It soon became clear that were I to give "individual" attention to the "retarded" pupils in my class, no progress would be possible.

That and other similar problems first hinted at the big disgrace that is Bantu Education. For many it gives no education, but is simply "going with those going" (*"Ukuhamba nabahambayo"*). Teachers just do not have enough time to help stragglers — they barely manage to forge ahead with the ones bright enough to make it with minimum instruction and minimum supervision. Minimum is all I could give, that thinly stretched I was.

"You and you and you . . . take out your Xhosa reading books and read Lesson 8, page 74, silently.

"All those who got more than three sums wrong, do your corrections and learn multiplication tables 7 and 8.

"Everyone who is standing, come and form a circle here in front!"

Dividing the pupils into working groups, each with a specific problem to work on, leaves me free to direct my total attention to the circle, now seated.

The circle is made up of pupils terribly backward in their arithmetic. After five (at least) years in school, these young people find it difficult to add and subtract (in the abstract).

Squatting, we draw circles wherein we put pebbles. The circles we call kraals; and the pebbles are labeled cattle. Each pupil has one small and one bigger kraal.

"Take three cows to visit the little kraal. Another four come visiting this three. How many cows are now in the little kraal?"

"Miss! Miss! Nomsa has passed wind!" interupts my remedial arithmetic teaching!

These seventy-two souls depended on me for Xhosa lessons; English lessons; lessons in Afrikaans; Health Education; Social Studies, Music, Arithmetic and Religious Instruction. In addition, I taught sewing to the girls and coached the two netball teams that the school had.

It was a rare night I wasn't bent over books, marking essays; marking grammar; marking arithmetic; marking spelling; marking, marking, marking.

On the whole, the children were heart-rending in their innocence and yet experience. They had seen too much, too soon. It was there in their shifty eyes and in their lies. It was in their deliberate but unconvincing use of suggestive words and in their too-innocent play. Childhood, though, showed its deep-rootedness: these children were, above all, just children; even on such barren soil they would grow.

For the first time, I began to understand why the older people say:

"Oh, I don't know why they have to grow up."

At that time the government subsidized education to the tune of R480 for a white child and R28 for an African child. It has not burdened the African child with compulsory education. (The currency changed from pounds sterling to rands and cents in 1961, at which time the pound was equivalent to two rands.)

Through my two years of teacher-training I had not once come across mention, verbal or written, of African teachers' salaries. Little wonder, seeing that the princely sum, £11.19s 11d (then about $48) greeted me when I entered the field.

People my age, who had not hindered thier progress in life by going to high school or teacher-training college, thus wasting five years in which they could have been earning, were making about the same amount of money as I was. They had been gaining experience while I had been studying. Fat help that had turned out to be. Besides, they had the added advantage of low operating costs. Who expects a domestic worker to turn out all dolled up, wearing stockings every day? Instead, she can save on clothing by wearing uniforms.

Except for the dubious honor of the prestige the job carries within the community, there was, I felt, very little to recommend the teaching profession; to Africans, that is.

The hours were long. The work was not done come end of the school day; far from it, what with games and matches to supervise. I never heard of a separate games' teacher until years later when I went to teach at a white school. Choir practice, usually after school.

Overcrowding was and still is rife, which augurs badly for the teacher-pupil ratio and leads to the "progression of the brightest" phenomenon: whereby the only pupils who learn are those so bright that even with minimum supervision they could probably make their way satisfactorily through the syllabus.

This, I felt, robs everyone. The bright student is held back; the not-too-bright student does not and cannot get the extra help she needs. The teacher too is robbed. I have found that it leaves a bad taste in a teacher's mouth to know that he or she was minimally effective. That those pupils who with encouragement could have made it, didn't.

Little solace can flow from the knowledge that one did one's best. One's best? The doubt lingers — one's best for which one? After all, even the most self-centered teacher must realize the ultimate beneficiary of our attempts has to be the pupil. And to choose, even indirectly, those who will succeed and those who will not succeed, is painful through the year but particularly when, come year end, the trusting little ones have to be let in on the secret: "You have passed"; "You have failed."

I have said or written these words to scores of children. All along, I had known the agony for which some were destined. Such is the design of the government. And such is the abetting by even those of us who regard ourselves as oppressed. Which we are. But we are also called upon to help in that oppression and unwittingly become instruments of it.

The first day of school, I was quite surprised when one pupil came up to me after morning assembly and asked, "You're a teacher?" in utter amazement. We had been neighbors at Zwelitsha, the township that was put up shortly after our home in Blaauvlei had been burnt down.

Not only had Philemon been my next-door neighbor, but we had been friends. We had played together, fought together and against each other. Yes, he had been behind me in school. Not only was I young for my class but most pupils during my time were much too old for the classes in which they were. This combination of factors had led to my beginning a teaching career at age nineteen when there were, in the school, young people twenty years and older. The same was true of other primary schools.

As I have said, there was no bus or train service between Guguletu, where I lived, and Nyanga, where I taught. As I didn't have and wasn't about to have a car, and knew no one who did, the only alternative was walking there and back. Some unwritten rule stipulated that women teachers wear high-heeled shoes and nylon stockings; winter or summer. It is therefore to this period of lofty dress-code that I attribute the numerous foot problems that afflict me today.

I know my parents and siblings were bursting with pride as I began teaching. Later I was to learn that African teachers, together with all other professional African people, make up but one per cent of their people. I know my own family did not then and do not now, know the statistical significance of my achievement, humble as that achievement was. However, given their very ordinary, indeed, powers of observation, given their knowledge of their own human world, they were aware a small miracle had taken place even if they did not use that word.

Utterly surprised and taken aback as I was by the realization of how far from lofty my salary as a teacher was going to be, my mind boggled at the sheer temerity of my father. I marveled at the courage of sending two children to high school and, later, one of those to a teacher-training college when, apparently, we were a slice of bread away from public assistance. Except, there was no public assistance for Africans.

It didn't take me long to figure out how little my father was earning. Long having taken it for granted that as he worked he was paid, I had not unduly worried my little head about the economics of my education. Once I joined the ranks of the employed, however, things changed.

If I had cause to complain about my salary, what could he be getting? If this was what educated people got, I thought, alarmed, what has he been earning all along? Poor father who worked from six o'clock in the morning until six o'clock in the evening — rain or shine, with no shelter from either, out there filling 'em up, changing flat tires, checking oil, wiping windows, windshields, and rear view mirrors, every day, six days a week; but what did he earn?

My own financial distress made me acutely aware of his, which had to be worse. My very sheltered upbringing, the conspiracy of silence of those teachers who had qualified before me and never murmured a word about their being underpaid, the incomplete preparation which took place when I was supposedly being prepared for the role of teacher, all these myths shattered. I couldn't believe the demands I had made on my uncomplaining parents while I was away at Keiskamahoek where I received my teacher training.

I would write asking for pocket money or an article of clothing. Two or three weeks of waiting was enough to trigger another letter querulous in tone and loud in criticism. My favorite jab had been, "Oh, I see you have dumped me here only to forget about me." To this day, ooh, how I wish I could eat those words.

Years later, I had the opportunity to work with a group of young teachers running a study center for high-school dropouts. The students at Inxaxheba Study Centre were, on the whole, well above average in intelligence. As they came for tutorials and had to discuss their work among themselves, rather than passively listen to a teacher, a degree of discipline, autonomy, and motivation was required.

Both students and teachers were enthusiastic. One of the factors, no doubt, Sr. Aine Hardiman's infectious and boundless optimism. An Irish Dominican nun, Sr. Aine had started the project and was responsible for its day-to-day running.

One of the three young men in this group, a gentle person soft-spoken and kindly disposed, was even handsome as well. He tutored the math classes, and was reputed to be a whiz at it.

Mbulelo (not his real name) had once entertained dreams of going to Wentworth Medical School. For reasons I never got to know, this dream he had had to put on hold, or, who knows, relinquish. I know, though, he was raised by a single parent — the mother. And he had a twin brother.

I had no idea where Mbulelo's twin brother was or what he was doing. Township families tend to exhibit such diversity in character it is sometimes prudent to make no unnecessary inquiries about the relatives of those with whom fate has, for this or that reason, temporarily joined you.

"Sis' Sindi," I heard Mbulelo address me one day. I was older, much older than the other teachers and all of them called me Sis' Sindi. So did the students.

The question in his voice, I gathered from the look on his face, meant did I have some time. I nodded; and he came and sat beside me.

"You know, Sis' Sinsi, something is bothering me." Lord, I thought, his girlfriend is pregnant and he doesn't know what to do. Marry her? Just pay the damages and not ask for her hand in marriage? Or, worse still, raced my fertile mind, he is not certain he is the father.

"I am a twin, you know, I have a brother. My twin brother. And I love him very much, Sis' Sindi.

"But this chap, he just won't listen to anybody. Mother is worried about him. As you know, we have no father. She raised us all on her own."

I was a little taken aback, for now I truly was in the dark. Ask him what was bothering him or ask him how he thought I could help? I dithered. And, so, the young man, reading my silence as a sign to continue, did just that:

"My brother, Sis' Sindi, has fallen in with the wrong crowd. Both my mother and I have tried to show him what he is doing is wrong. But he does not listen to us."

I knew then, what this personable young and promising lad was going through. We Xhosa people believe twins have a special bond, stronger than that between mere siblings. When one twin "cracks open" ("*liqhezuke*"), before his or her coffin is lowered into the grave, it is first lowered into the grave with the surviving twin in it. It is only after this mock burial that the real burial takes place. That is the custom. Twins are not separated, even by death. Each ceremony undergone by one, the other has to go through; if, as circumstances sometimes demand, in mock fashion, pretending or going through the motion but not the reality of the experience. Such, for example, is the case during the circumcision of the male twin in a set of mixed-sex twins.

Mbulelo was suffering the degradation of the morale and morals of his other self. His brother had become one of a group of shoplifters.

"This morning," said he in a low voice, so low I had to strain hard to catch what he was saying, "I said to him, 'Tamsanqa, do you realize you'll end up in jail?'

"Do you know what he said, to me Sis' Sindi? He said, 'When I'm *in* jail and when I'm *out* of jail, I'm going to make sure there's a difference.' That's what he said to me, Sis' Sindi."

The brother had then gone on to inform Mbulelo that *he* was the one in danger of wasting his life: "You are in jail right now. Except, you don't even know it." Tamsanqa (Luck) had said to Mbulelo (Thanks).

3

Yes, teachers' salaries, a decade and a half after I had started teaching, were still so low as to elicit scorn from everybody, from lowly domestic workers to common criminals. When I had entered the field of education, to say I had been astounded at the pittance African teachers earned would be an understatement.

If my eyes were still being opened by tales such as Mbulelo's, it was not because I lacked experience. No sooner had I started teaching than I had two basic, if hard lessons: as I've mentioned before, I learnt that a certificate confirming my competence and expertise was no guarantee of (i) a job, or (ii) meaningful remuneration.

A jolting lesson came three months after I began my proud teaching career. Had I consulted an oracle in April when I got my teaching post, I might have heard: "This is your house of fertility." Unbeknown to me, that month, it was not just what I thought of as my long, arduous, and rigorous training that had borne fruit.

"When last have you been sick?" I looked at the love of my life as if he had taken leave of his senses.

"I don't mean sick-sick, you know? . . . You know how girls get their . . . ?"

After a brief hushed discussion (although we were alone) we realized I had to be pregnant.

"Three months," announced the doctor. This was July and I had been teaching for all of four months.

In 1962 very little was known in my part of the world about contraception. Certainly, what little African women my age group knew was positively dangerous. We are a group which, as young people, was caught up in transition, with sex having been reduced to a small "gold" band minus apprenticeship and spontaneity. Previously, sex education for adolescents had been a fact of life. Both boys and girls were taught sex play that satisfied their urges with no risk of their

TO MY CHILDREN'S CHILDREN

being plunged into roles of parenthood prematurely. Then came the missionaries; and sex disappeared from the agenda of educating the young. All very well; except that the natural urges refused to succumb to civilization or Christianity and go away.

The sun took flight, forsaking the sky. My personal tragedy was a family disaster. Father had suffered scorn and ridicule for educating a girl child. I had done exactly what his tormentors had predicted. My parents had borrowed money; they had done without so I could get an education and not suffer the way they did; they had even dabbled in the not altogether legal. And how had I repaid them? Had I worked for them even a year? ONE year?

As is customary when calamity of such proportions befalls a family, relatives far and near were notified; our daughter is spoiled. She is heavy (with child). The only difference between what followed this disaster and what would have ensued had someone died, was that those relatives farther away than a day's journey by train only wrote letters or otherwise sent word, commiserating with my parents on their loss. And no one actually wore all black, the color of mourning.

Funeral-faced relatives came. Some, during the week, usually at night, because most of them worked. Most came over the weekend, for the same reason. Tears were shed, mostly by women; although a few men shed some too. Tears were shed until my own well dried up. Completely. I was cried out.

I continued going to school and my stomach continued lying, remaining a mocking virginal flat. Even I was often assailed by happy, if brief, moments of doubt. How could I be pregnant with a waistline this trim? I'd ask myself. Right up to the seventh month I could have modeled swimwear for a *Vogue* catalogue.

After consultations, three men were chosen and sent to the address I had given. Mindful, still, of my standing within the community, these human summonses did not go there during the day. And, which was a godsend, went there without the benefit of the spoiled goods, me, leading the way. It is the custom in such cases to have a small group of men, in broad daylight, with sticks in their hands, follow some miserable-looking young woman, the fallen maiden, to the home of the offender.

She it is who is spoiled. Therefore, since she had reported no rape,

97

she must lead those who would seek redress or vengeance on behalf of her disgraced and cheated family. A voluntary accessory during the act, she now leads these men of her family to the rogue, her accomplice, for she is the instrument of the downfall of her family. She has to be willing to give the evidence that will lead to the restoration of its good name and fallen fortunes. To redeem herself, in their eyes, she must be a willing instrument of the family's redemption in the eyes of the community.

But I, being a teacher, suffered no such public humiliation. Society rests solidly on its pillars. When those pillars display cracks, everything possible is done to mend them. That not possible, society is at pains to conceal those cracks. Even as a twig on which nothing much rested, I benefited immensely from this unwritten rule. Which is not to say I escaped all censure: NO.

At school I was doing well. The principal lavished compliments on me. Our netball team became the talk of the other teams. Awesome. And I was the coach.

I had started teaching with an exaggerated air of maturity. However, there was still a lot of the child in me. I loved playing; and as I coached, I would often get into the field and play. The kids thought this was a great joke and we had fun. But after the news that I was pregnant, I played in earnest, frantically attempting to recapture my childhood. A childhood I was painfully aware was running out as fast as the child within me grew, relentlessly, towards its own birth.

A complication, perhaps embarrassment would be a more appropriate word, was that the gentleman in question did not have lobola, the bride price my parents expected in return for their educated daughter's hand. Women far less educated were fetching lobola of two to five hundred rand from their suitors. In my parents' (and, indeed others') eyes, my value had increased with the education I had received. And here I had the misfortune or stupidity, depending on where your sympathies lay, of allowing myself to be spoiled by a migrant laborer, a man who, at any given time of day, any day of the month, could have his pockets turned inside out with no danger of littering the streets of Guguletu with coins.

The school was going on tour during the September school vacation.

Although I had resigned my post, I left with the tour. But I went only as far as Port Elizabeth; there, I went to one of Luthando's relatives who, he had assured me, expected me. I had left all that to him.

I needed to be away from my parents, from Jongi, from my younger, adoring siblings; and even from relatives, friends, and neighbors. The wound I had inflicted on them was too raw for me to watch, daily, as they bled.

My parents had been under the impression I was going with the tour and would return, therefore, before schools reopened. I wrote telling them of my plans. Plans? All I had really thought out was putting distance between myself and them; removing myself from the obvious pain I had caused. That I was burdening the poor woman, herself childless, who suddenly found herself fostering a grown woman, one about to be a mother, I woke up to only after her far from warm reception. I belatedly saw that I had not really given much thought to the plan.

What do you propose to do about prenatal care? What did Luthando say you would do for food? Where are your parents? Did Luthando not see that your parents can have him arrested? Thick and fast fell questions I had not anticipated.

Mother replied, by telegram: *"Sindiwe Buya."* ("Sindiwe return.") Luthando's relative needed no second bidding. The very next day she bundled me into a third-class compartment of the train. I had wasted money, running away, for all of two weeks.

Back home, I sensed a slight change in my parents' attitude. My little escapade, I was to learn years later, had not only upset them. It had scared them into asking each other, "What if, instead of running away she had done something else? Something worse?"

Even when my mother told me about this years later, the alternative course of action was not given a name. Maybe it was too awful, too gruesome, to be borne in my poor parents' minds. But if what they thought is what I think they thought, then they do not know their daughter. I used to have a middle name which, for reasons best left alone, I dropped. But sometimes I think the C that would have been my middle initial could very well have stood for Coward. I am a confessing coward. All who know me know this unpalatable truth about me. I tell it freely for fear it will, anyway, come out.

Since it was not unusual for African teachers beginning a new job to go on without pay for anything between three and six months, I had received my first check in September. It was quite a fat one as it retroactively covered my salary from April to date.

As expected, I gave the money to father. Now, I had returned from Port Elizabeth and was "his burden." I turned my head to preparations for the baby's coming and Luthando helped with the layette and other incidentals. However, it was hard going.

Midway through the pregnancy, father reconsidered the situation and came to a compromise, a traditional Xhosa ceremony: traditional, minus the frills. This involves the husband to be undertaking to pay lobola at some future date. Meanwhile, negotiators from both families met, discussed, and came to agreement. All very sensible and practical seeing as the sealing of the relationship had been done already.

Token lobola was offered and accepted. A sheep was slaughtered. The ceremony followed soon thereafter, and I was taken to my new home. We were man and wife. I wore the traditional German print dress and apron (in ankle length to depict my status). A black head scarf, low over my eyes, a shawl over the shoulders, completed the picture.

A young wife. An expectant mother. No longer employed. I was a housewife. Less than a year after leaving St. Matthew's with the certainty, at least in my own mind, that a splendid career was beckoning, I was a housewife. Nothing more. Nothing less.

No feminist, I had nonetheless often joked with colleagues at St. Matthew's: "I was born for better things than washing shirts and mending socks." In my clear eyes, I had fallen. Fallen far short of what I had dreamt of becoming. But I could see now way out of the quagmire in which, even as I watched myself wallow, I sank deeper and ever deeper, with each passing day.

As a primapara, I should have been booked into a hospital for the confinement. As one who had done nothing about her pregnancy till her seventh month, I could only engage the services of a midwife. "You're too late to get in at any of the maternity hospitals," one of the nurses at the Guguletu Prenatal Clinic had enlightened me.

Another outcome of the kind of sex education, if you can call it that, I had received, was that, even at this late stage, the birth process was still somewhat of a mystery to me. I had heard of women screaming, breaking furniture, calling out to the beasts, the men who had inflicted the pregnancy on them. In the throes of giving birth, they called on them so they could kill them for making them go through such agony. Alone. It was with much trepidation that I awaited my turn in that special hell for women.

Therefore, the morning I woke up feeling a slight heaviness not unlike that announcing the advent of my periods, I took little notice. I suffered severe period pains as a young woman. What I felt that morning, compared to what I was used to, really hardly registered as pain. Never mind labor pains.

By evening, I happened to mention this to mother who had popped in for a quick visit. This was only her second visit in the two months since I had returned from Port Elizabeth. Her visits, when they did take place, could only be furtive. No mother flaunts a daughter's changed status when that daughter's being a wife entails no gain. Why had she been raising such a daughter? To give her away? She was risking father's wrath and communal criticism for appearing to condone what I had done.

Mother, herself veteran of eight live deliveries and at least one miscarriage I have vague recollections of — I have never heard it mentioned except when it was actually happening and immediately thereafter — sent for the midwife.

Mrs. Kobi, a woman of my clan (MamTolo), a popular midwife, was, fortunately, home. The messenger's chest was still heaving from the sprinting there and back when the nurse came. I had known Mrs. Kobi or Dad'oBawo (aunt on father's side) since my childhood days in Blaauvlei. She was brusque and businesslike, and, like my family, she was Anglican. And since she was a Tolo, we were related and she had always shown me that special attention due to a niece. Tonight, however, I saw a professional, a health-care giver.

She scrubbed, examined me, and announced: "You should have had this baby a long time ago." I was stupefied as she added, "I don't like this."

As she muttered to herself about "head . . . engaged" and something that was "too high," I retreated into myself. Mrs. Kobi then announced she was returning to her house from where she could phone for the ambulance. Mother hovered anxiously. Hands wringing. I saw she was nervous. I was so calm, dazed. It was as if the whole thing was happening to someone else, and I was merely watching, an idle spectator.

Even as I was taken on a stretcher to the lights-flashing ambulance, I could not shake off the air of unreality that blanketed me and the evening's events. That I was, after all, on my way to a hospital (I didn't know which), just added to the dream-like quality of the proceedings.

Somerset Hospital is in Mouille Point. And that is where I found myself. In the emergency ward.

No sooner was I transferred from ambulance to bed or examining table than I was surrounded by a horde of white-coated men. One of them, the teacher, in my grasp of the situation, began teaching the others. Showing them what I gathered were the incongruencies of my case. Apparently, broad feet and large hands do not often go with contracted pelvis, which was the condition I gathered I exhibited. A condition that was to save me from the horrors of natural delivery.

With one hand cupped and the other rolled into a fist, the teacher-doctor demonstrated to the group a maneuver they were going to try. Describing, with the two hands thus held, something like a ball and socket joint, he showed them how, by easing the lubricated ball out of the socket at an angle, it was sometimes possible to deliver "disproportionate" cases naturally.

I tell you, I was very lucid. Then they made me count or smell something, there my memory becomes a little hazy, although I do remember this:

There I am, as big as a balloon, the flying kind, stark naked, surrounded by white medical men; did that stop my vanity? One of the doctors says, "She is small." And another responds, "Yes, small but petite." To which I glow all over.

As I knew no French, although I had some vague idea that small and petite were synonymous, I can only conclude that it was more the tone of voice than my grasp of the nuances and subtleties that conveyed the compliment contained in *"petite." Mais oui, ça m'a beaucoup plu.*

The next I knew, I was lying on my back in a strange bed. Gingerly, I moved my head from side to side. Rows and rows of women in narrow white-clothed beds jumped into my eyes. I was in a hospital ward, as my senses returned, I remembered.

My right hand woke up. Down, slowly it traveled downwards. It reached my tummy and surprised a slightly flabby empty flatness there. And I knew the life that had blown me up till my toes were strangers to my eyes had assumed a separateness. Was no longer mine to help live. Not in the dire and absolute desperation of the past nine months. No. It could go on living even if I were to die. It could live, given supportive conditions.

My eyes began to feel at home in the strange room. There were women, some nursing infants, some asleep, some sitting up, others chatting, and a few out of their beds, walking about. Later, days later, I noticed red-eyed women. Tearstained women. I'm glad to say, few in number.

For six months I had fantasized. He or she would look like me or him. Maybe he or she would have my eyes and his mouth. I had been consistently considerate in dealing out physical features. He or she would get the best from each of us. Six long months I'd played a god.

The bright pink, chubby little person, wound in unfamiliar hospital swaddling, set my heart aflutter. She was none of the configurations I'd carried tenderly (if secretly and a little guiltily) within me. She looked not at all like me and resembled not at all her father.

Stories of baby changes flashed before me. What if this is not my child quickly turned from question to horrified certainty.

Caesarean section, a marvelous way of giving birth, has this one drawback. The mother is not witness to the birth of her child. At least, that was the case then. These days, I hear, it is possible for the mother, anaesthetized locally, actually to be wide awake, alert, and watching the procedure.

The air of disbelief was to accompany the birth of each of my three children as they were all delivered in the same manner. Fortunately, the magic of holding a baby in my own arms, having it tug, piglet-like, from my teat, its pulsating fontanelle affirming it lives, soon sweeps aside doubt.

It was the first visiting hour for fathers that showed me a gruesome grief. A man and a woman. She, in bed, sitting up. He stands next to her bed. Something about the way he just stands there, not sitting down, not brushing his lips against her proffered cheek, her NOT proffered cheek, pulls my attention to the pair. They are shrouded in malaise; united by some invisible but tangible steel-like web, the weight of which droops the man's shoulders. The woman, half-turned away from him, has her head hanging. Concentrated sorrow. Empty arms. Filled breasts, dripping teats. And no one to suckle. Unfulfilled expectations. Stillbirth. From a mother's eyes, stream the tears her baby would never shed.

Then I learnt the secret of mothers everywhere from time immemorial: to each mother, her baby is perfection. I had not once entertained the possibility of a defect; never mind a lifeless form. Thembeka may not have looked like anything my feeble brain had imagined, but by the time we left the hospital, I was absolutely convinced of her beauty, nay, perfection. That others confirmed my opinion was a mere incidental. If they had told me she looked like Frankenstein's bride, I would not have believed them.

Thembeka and I returned home, to my parents' house, by ambulance. And as the ambulance attendant, baby in arms, escorted me to the house, mother, who must have been waiting hovering around the window, stepped out of the house. She received the baby, thanked the attendant, and turned around to face the doorway. The attendant had not reached the ambulance before the baby was given her very first African ceremony: made to enter her home (*ukumngenisa ekhaya*). The baby, swaddling and all, was placed at the threshold. Then mother, all the time talking to her, picked her up and walked inside, the baby tenderly against her breast. The two have been extremely close from that day. Unwanted babies are a foreign concept in African tradition. Unwanted pregnancies, yes, but not unwanted children.

Father had not come to see us at the hospital. That surprised me little. I loved my father very much, but I would be lying if I said he was a demonstrative man. How we knew he loved us, is still a mystery to me. But of that we were convinced. Even now, nearly two decades after his passing away, we, his children often talk lovingly about him. And I also have come to accept that I will always miss him. I do.

When he returned from work that evening, he came into the bedroom where I, the new mother (*umdlezana*), was in bed, the baby next to me. Gruffly, he greeted and quickly demanded to see "this thing of yours."

As his gaze lingered on his first grandchild, however, I spied a little of what lay beyond the furrowed, brooding brow; beyond the often hooded eyes: the deep, abiding tenderness trapped inside a body that had never had or seen or felt that sentiment directed to itself. Father had grown up fatherless, his own father having been swallowed by the gold mines of (eGoli) Johannesburg.

Mother could not do enough for me. And here I was a willing, if not eager, beneficiary of two things — my own inborn tendency towards laziness and mother's great respect for operations. Since I had had the baby by operation, and since the understanding, certainly in the African townships, is that one who has undergone such an ordeal should be spared any other, mother forbade me the slightest exertion.

The baby's napkins were washed by others. The baby herself was bathed by mother who, I suspect, would not have trusted even me with that delicate task; even had I not been "weak from the operation."

It was with great reluctance, therefore, that six weeks after our return from hospital, I was allowed to return to Luthando. I welcomed this move because, although I have said I enjoyed the fuss that was being made of me, I have another fear about operations.

When I was at St. Matthew's Teacher Training College, there was a student, a girl a few years older than me. Rain or shine, winter or summer, Nozimbo had her greatcoat on.

A tall, willowy girl, she always, always, looked tired. Her eyes wore a weariness as though she had borrowed them from her great-grandmother who had seen the Battle of the Axe. Her long, thin legs carried her, step by tottering step, as if she were a new-born kid goat or a goat recovering from a severe bout of bronchitis. They trembled, threatening to buckle under her thin frame that could not have weighed much. Stooped rounded shoulders protested their perpetual burdening: "Why should we carry pounds of wool, every day you continue to live?" I imagined their daily refrain.

When we had been newcomers and her condition could still be

attributed to nervousness or journey fatigue, some had ventured the question: "What happened to you?" Swift, the answer had come: "I had an operation."

Appendix, is what had ailed her. I remember saying to myself maybe she would have been better off had she remained with the illness. In my opinion then, she had benefited naught from the cure, the operation. But then, that was the opinion of an eighteen-year-old, with not a grain of sand's worth of medical expertise.

Some good did come of poor Nozimbo's condition: if ever I undergo an operation, I had vowed to myself, I will be ever so careful afterwards, very careful so as to mend completely. And then, I will continue my life as if I had not had that operation.

Two months after Thembeka's birth, I started living as though I had not had an operation. I refused to be a victim of something that was supposed to help me, cure me.

A motif I had sensed with the simplicity of a child reappeared, in sharper focus. Unyielding. Unforgiving. It was to recur, time and time again as my life unfolded into early, middle, and now, advanced middle adulthood. Christians find it very difficult to forgive the frailty of others. Judgmental comes to mind. Judgmental and condemnatory.

If my parents were devastated, our relatives were as loud in their criticism as they had been in their praise when I had passed the final year teachers' training course. For some strange reason, the men, my uncles on both sides of the family, were more vocal about how I had let father down. And, of course, mother too. And after all they had done for me.

It helped but little that I was full of self-censure, daily flagellating myself. And then Uncle Sithembele, who had never struck me as particularly sensitive, surprised me. He worked at a garage in Sea Point. The baby, Thembeka, was a few weeks old when he came on a visit.

"Ninjani, Sindi?" ("How are you [pl.], Sindi?"). I gave my now usual and clearly far from jubilant answer. I was still cautious not to display too glad a mien. People might interpret that to mean I was proud of what I had done. Are we allowed to rejoice in the results of our errors?

Uncle Sithembele asked, *"Lunjani usana?"* ("How is the baby?")

And I hadn't answered that question when, without raising a brow, with no lowering of voice nor change of tone, his hand fished out a rand note from his pocket. Giving the money to me, he said, *"Uya kuzithengela isephu."* ("You will buy yourself soap.") Soap, the metonymy, in Xhosa, for sundries or necessities. The Department of Bantu Education, as it was then called, did not recognize traditional liaisons. In the eyes of officialdom, therefore, I was not married.

I was not married in the eyes of the church either. My perfect baby was dry and out of napkins by her first birthday. She already walked. Healthy, she taught me nothing about childhood illnesses. I breast-fed her for six months and felt her cutting her teeth that way. But my own siblings had been christened, without fail, long before they even learned to crawl. Thembeka's baptism had had to be put on hold.

By the time the baby was three months old, the restriction imposed by unemployment was killing me. A teaching job was out of the question, for at least two years — the "punishment" meted out to fallen women teachers like me.

I began job-hunting. I took buses to get to public telephone booths — in Lansdowne, Claremont, Rylands, or Athlone. The few phones in Guguletu were invariably out of order. On the very rare occasions they weren't, that miracle was announced by the long queues next to them. I phoned, in response to advertisements in newspapers: hotels, hospitals, restaurants, and factories. No luck. I could not get a job as a waitress or scullerymaid. I could not find one as a nurse-aid or cleaner. Jobs as a tea-girl eluded me.

Eventually, desperate, I resorted to domestic work.

4

I worked as a domestic servant for four years, during which time I was a "part of" four households. First, a British family. The husband was in the navy and had been posted to Youngsfield, Cape Town.

Then there was the elderly Jewish couple who lived in the prestigious suburb of Oranjezicht. This was the most fastidious family and the medem here the stingiest and the most suspicious human being I have ever had the misfortune to encounter. She is the epitome of the white South African often depicted in township lore: one who looks at Africans in the knowing manner that warns she is not fooled by any outward semblance of respectability; is gifted with ability to smell a thief under any guise.

This lady worked mornings. She left home about eight o'clock and returned shortly after one in the afternoon. The family had a gigantic double-story house that had, at least, four bedrooms. They had a two-car garage which had two cars in it. They had a lovely garden at the front of their house and sizable backyard with the usual paraphernalia. I cannot say this house was sparsely furnished. The master owned a thriving construction company before South Africa knew the word inflation and when depression was qualified by "great" to refer to the economy of the United States in the era before World War II.

After this family I worked for a Greek family who owned a large restaurant in Cape Town. When I applied for this job the husband told me I wouldn't be required to cook: not even for myself! What he didn't tell me was that for years after I had left them I would not even want to look at curry and I would be suspicious of all restaurant food.

Lastly, there were the Koorns, from whom I would be "rescued" by my husband, a good four years after I had embarked on this form of livelihood.

The Garlands were British and had not immigrated to South Africa. They were there on service to Her Majesty the Queen. Families such as this one paid the going rate for servants and housed them in the servants' quarters they themselves had not built, but had found attached to the houses they rented or bought. By the transitory nature of their sojourn, they cannot but be different from the ordinary employer in South Africa: Mrs. Garland allowed me the use of her library. My baby was allowed to stay with me and, during the day, if she wakened, could be brought into the house rather than being left alone in the maid's room, behind the house.

I had presented myself for an interview following a telephone conversation. Mrs. Garland had placed an ad in the morning paper, the *Cape Times*. She had advertised for a "colored cook-general with contactable references." Twenty rands a month seemed, to me, an appropriate wage, but for reasons quite different from those Mrs. Garland had in mind. This was the going rate for a servant of average ability.

My heart thumped in my mouth as she opened the door to my ring.

"Cynthia?"

"Yes, M'em."

"Well, come in and tell me, have you worked before?"

I had come to see this lady out of desperation. I was none of the things she sought: I am African and not a person of mixed descent, so-called colored according to government classification and labeling in South Africa. I had no references, never mind "contactable" ones! And the reason for that was the very simple one that I had never worked as a domestic servant before.

Without actually lying, I must have convinced her that it would be to our mutual benefit were she to employ me. That is what she did. To be sure, I had a lot going for me, as far as domestic servants go! I did not drink: her liquor was safe. I did not smoke: her supply of cigars and cigarettes was safe. I had no record of pilfering, thanks to my extreme shyness of the jail system. I was suitably humble, every pore of my being exuding humility and eagerness to serve. When she asked me what faults she might expect from me were she to give me the job, I frankly revealed my great weakness for books!

"M'em, sometimes M'em might find something not done because I was reading."

"That my friends who have maids who steal their food, drink, money and wear their clothes on the sly should thus be blessed" written all over her face, she offered me the job there and then, although we both had doubts as to my ability to do it.

I had to promise, to myself, never to give evidence of the numerous other faults I had not confessed to possessing.

Mr. and Mrs. Garland had two sons. Each had been born on some non-British soil, a result of the nature of their father's profession. Looking back, I now know these children were being brought up in a manner not typically white South African: undoubtedly, a preparation for their eventual return to a world where racism does not carry the government's stamp of approval.

Christopher and Ian, aged eight and six, respectively, were children with all that that entails. They were no saints, to be sure. But, on the other hand, neither were they devilish brats. And, what is more important, as we say in the African townships, they were being brought up. Most white children in South Africa simply grow up. There is no pruning, no tending, weeding or nurturing. They pick up, as the years roll relentlessly on, whatever prevailing societal attitudes, whims and mannerisms might be in the offing. Hence the singularly incestuous political inbreeding in that bleeding land.

The Garland boys were encouraged to do some chores in the home, despite the existence of a maid. They addressed me by name instead of "nanny." They were respectful, most of the time; and discipline was sure and swift when they were found to have been remiss.

As I have indicated, this was my first job in domestic service. I had a lot to learn. I learnt it. I even learnt to turn out a creaseless starched white shirt for the CO (the husband was the Commanding Officer at Youngsfield Military Base) - no mean feat for one who had never, until then, used any electrical appliance!

Mr. and Mrs. Garland had wanted a "colored cook-general." Although they were not highly conversant with the color-layered differential system promulgated by the South African government, I had been honest with them about my being "Bantu" or African. "General" maybe I was; but "cook" I decidedly was not, as Madam Garland was soon to find out. However, I fancied she was getting a fair bargain as I am of very sober habits! In all the time I would work for her, she would never have a care about a crime being committed in her home by me, or with my aiding and abetting. This is more than a lot of employers, be it in kitchen work or industry, mine or farm, could hope for.

Those who see themselves as perpetually and effectively excluded from an adequate livelihood often find ways of redressing the wrong. The underpaid of South Africa must have, for, given the excuses for wages most earn, they would not be alive to laugh about it had they not somehow found a way, good or bad, legal or not, to redistribute some of the wealth locked in white hands.

I was taught by Mrs. Garland to cook: stews, roasts, soups, fried fish and fish frikkadels, cottage pie, and a host of other dishes besides. She taught me how to lay the table with proper arrangement of the cutlery, from outside inwards. She had to start with telling me the difference between meat- and fish- and butter-knives and forks! She taught patiently and I learnt eagerly.

It is here that I first encountered what was to become, later on and with other employers, a veritable bane:

A sense of inadequacy would engulf me when, upon medem's return from a trip to the hairdresser or the dentist or bridge or bowls, tennis, swimming, squash, or whatever, I would report:

"M'em, a lady came to see you and said she'd phone later on."

"Who was it?"

"She said she was your friend, m'em!" I'd reply, thinking, "Awu, who ever heard of a white lady giving a black woman her name?"

"Was she fair or dark?" me'm would ask, little realizing she might as well ask me to decipher the hieroglyphics!

"Heela, are there dark white people?" I would think.

"She was white, me'm. A European." Thinking, "She knows she only has white friends! What does she want from me?"

"Oh, don't be so stupid! Of course she was a European, but . . ." hesitatingly, thinking of a way of gleaning information from the certifiable idiot in her employ, her "girl," me . . .

"Was the lady . . . eh . . . you know . . . was she . . . very very light or not so very very light?"

Why didn't I just tell her that to my unschooled eye, all white folk looked very very white to me. That I did not have the skills to distinguish between a blonde and a brunette? That her questions mystified me and put her, in my mind, in a group I had begun suspecting of being headed for the loony bin! At that time I did not even know the words brunette and blonde.

I grew up living among my own people where everyone, except the occasional albino, has black hair, very dark brown eyes, and brown skin, in varying shades of brownness, shades I was to discover later, medem and her ilk could not distinguish. And I was in my thirties before anyone explained to me the trick whites use to distinguish between themselves. This also explained to me why white people looked the same to me. I had not been busy looking at the color of people's eyes or the color of their hair. NO.

To date, although I have managed to become a little adept at making these distinctions, I would never bet my money on my remembering what color so-and-so's eyes are if I am not looking at those eyes as I hazard the guess! Either I haven't noticed or I don't remember. Well, many are the insults I suffered for my disability.

Once Mrs. Garland had trained me to her satisfaction, life became reasonably calm. I knew what was expected of me and did it to the best of my ability. The day began at six-thirty in the morning and that fact was ensured by the simple expediency of an alarm clock. Next to the uniform the maid wears, the alarm clock is the most important constant in her work life. As she leaves the kitchen for the night, one of the last things the medem does is to give her the alarm clock wound and set for waking her up the next morning, at the appropriate time.

Thus at seven o'clock, freshly scrubbed and beuniformed, I unlocked the back door which led to the kitchen. Fifteen minutes later, shoulders braced, carrying a heavily laden tray, up the stairs I'd go to deliver the morning coffee to Master and Me'm Garland and the freshly squeezed orange juice to the boys. At seven-thirty, like clockwork, the family would descend to breakfast, orders for that having been given when I'd gone up to give them their coffee or orange juice in bed: scrambled eggs for one or two; with any luck more or all would want the same thing! A rare treat, for me. Usually it was:

"Make mine scrambled!"

"I want mine poached!"

"Boil mine, please."

"Oh, I feel like fried! And, could I have another glass of orange juice?"

"Say, 'please'!"

"Please!"

or:

"Two fried, sunny-side up."

"I want oats and a boiled egg."

"Please, make me two very light slices of toast!"

"Me too, me too!"

Fortunately, as much of the preparation for the mad morning rush was done the night before, shoes polished, pants pressed, shirts checked for spots and missing buttons, etc., the flurry would soon be over. Father and sons disappeared into the car and sped away, he to toil and they to learn.

Mrs. Garland would then begin her day, directing the maid regarding the day's work. Every day except Saturday, when I was half day off, and Sunday, when I came in only to help with breakfast and preparing the vegetable M'em would use for lunch, there was a special task over and above what I did every day: "Monday: laundry; washing and ironing. Tuesday: turn out and polish living- and dining-room. Wednesday: silver and brass polishing and anything else that needs shining. Thursday: kitchen and bathrooms; walls washing, stove and fridge cleaning, floors scrubbing. Friday: change bed linen and polish bedroom furniture and vacuum through entire floor, upstairs and downstairs. And mind you don't forget the stairs!"

A garden "boy" came twice a week and, fortnightly, washed the windows and the stoep.

Thus, an ordinary week wasn't that bad. I worked from seven in the morning to eight-thirty at night, Monday to Friday; and seven to two-thirty in the afternoon on Saturday; and Sunday, eight to ten-thirty. No, it wasn't a bad job for a domestic servant. Moreover, I had my baby with me, a luxury and a privilege. Most domestic workers are sleep-ins: they live on the premises. The law forbids members of their families, including spouses, to live with them. Some employers will turn a blind eye to the glaring signs indicating the frequent visits of a spouse: booming, obviously male voice, heavy footsteps in the middle of the night and the same steps, now departing, at crack of dawn; the heaped plate or, indeed, two plates carried by the maid to her room at night; the maid's laundry hanging on her wash line, shirts several sizes too large for her, man's underpants, etc. The law says it is forbidden, the wise employer may choose not to see the black man walking in her very yard! That the Garlands let me keep my baby with me made me see them as kinder than most and for that favor I would tolerate many an infringement!

It was when my employers entertained that I died!

These were the occasions that all but obliterated an already fragile self-confidence: the kettle of boiling water the hostess, medem, thrusts into my fumbling hand ordering me to take it inside and offer to the people, her guests. Fully convinced of the strange, not to say different, ways of white people, I go around offering "hot water me'm, hot water master" to anyone who has no cup in hand; knowing that something I couldn't quite lay my finger on was not tallying. Why didn't I know or guess the water was meant for those who had cups and found the beverage of their choice too strong for their liking? But then again, where would I have learnt such finesse? Where I grew up, we brewed tea, using the same tea leaves until the water emerged from the spout virtually undyed!

But that was nothing to the pushy guest who would demand something I couldn't make out, either because the speech was slurred from having had too much to drink or because he or she insisted on speaking with the mouth closed. The abuse I got when I didn't understand the request! I hid my resentment well, for domestic-worker lore has it that the servant may be right but she cannot be more right than a friend of the employer; which is to say, I realized, even with employers I regarded as somewhat more humane than the average employer, that the word of a white person is weightier than that of a black person employed by another white person!

However, bad as that sounds, nothing beat the guest who became too familiar, overstepping not only the boundaries of servant and employer classes, unbecoming as that may be, but overstepping racial or color lines — and that was illegal! Somehow, and this happened only once to me while I was working for this family, a servant is left with the bad aftertaste of having, even unknowingly, invited the unwanted attention. The feeling of shame at having made a spectacle of oneself — for how could a black woman, a servant, begin to think of herself as an object of desire when she was hard put to it going on believing that she was more than a beast of burden?

Clumsy fumbling hands that touched beyond the black ones outstretched in offering; hot sweet sour smell pouring from slack lips; glazed unseeing eyes as of dead fish; all this brought on a panic attack in the maid caught between fear of discovery and nagging doubt that she ought to be seeking such discovery to ward off this, this . . . thing! Doubt. Who would believe she wasn't the aggressor-instigator? Hell!

It was at this household that I graduated to "house" living. The mud huts, called rondavels, I had been born into belong to another world, another era; the succession of tin shacks I came to inhabit, having moved from village to town, were, if anything, a degradation after the rondavels, human sties! Being human, we'd made valiant but vain attempts to make houses of them. The attempts were bound to fail, meant to fail.

At the Garlands I deciphered the miracle of toilet paper! Any paper is a rare commodity in the villages of South Africa. Newspapers, bought and read by white employers do, however, end up in the locations. The numerous uses we who live in the locations and townships of South Africa have found for newspaper would amaze the uninitiated. Among these is that of toilet paper. Needless to say, seeing that proper toilet paper never came near our homes, there was no need for the gadget which keeps the paper suspended in a nook in the wall as if by some magic. Come to think of it, our bucket toilet system had been built without nook. This is in the locations and later, townships of Cape Town! Clearly, the use of toilet paper was not included in the planning of black South Africa's residential areas; not even the massive soulless complexes built in the government's great slum-clearance drive of the fifties and sixties — structures built with toilets — had a nook in those toilets!

One of the extras I used to do for this family was reading the children to sleep. This task, clearly outside the scope of our verbal contract, did not bring me any extra money. It necessitated my spending an hour or two of my own time "in the kitchen," metonym for being on duty inside the house. However, the recognition that I could read, that I was capable of higher duty, that I was not limited to sweeping, scrubbing, scouring, and steam-ironing; in short, that I, although a servant, had a brain, did a lot for my battered and bruised ego. It more than compensated for the absence of pecuniary gain.

When this family left, I had not really learnt the meaning of being a domestic servant. Only subsequently did I come across the strange customs such as the use of the third person when an employer, in addressing a servant, refers to herself or himself. "Madam" she will say, "wants tea. Madam is going shopping. If Master phones, tell

Master Madam will be back around three o'clock."

Surely, a game? I played along. But when it came to madams and masters referring to their offspring, some of whom were six or seven years old, as "master" and "miss," in the vain hope I would imitate that behavior, I'm afraid I must have been a great disappointment. I stubbornly refused to play along, balking at medeming and mistering anyone who did not pay my meager wages.

Oranjezicht is a small suburb nestling at the foot of Table Mountain in Cape Town. Its discreet houses hide behind high hedges of evergreen shrubs. Passing by, you may surprise a large-sounding dog or hear a splash as a swimmer slices into a pool.

The Goldbergs must have been in their late fifties. Their married son, a medical doctor, was away but I never found out where. I saw a lot of his pregnant wife, though. She lived in nearby Sea Point. Their divorced daughter and her pre-teenaged son lived with them. And that came as a surprise later on my first day there.

This was verily a close-knit family. And I found that burdensome.

Mrs. Goldberg's thing was her kitchen sink. During my induction she had quietly said, "Whatever you do, please look after my sink." I was to learn the seriousness of this request on the mercifully few occasions she had to haul me back to the kitchen in the middle of the night because she had, upon returning home from some party or function, family gathering or emergency, found the sink not as she liked it to be: spotlessly clean; dry; gleaming. With the ornaments, silver, brass, glass, copper, she kept arranged, just so, in that just so symmetrical order around the sink.

"I don't want my sink to rust," she would chide.

Despite the fact that she was the madam and I was the maid, she often made me feel I was stronger than she was. Not physically. She had this air of fearfulness that was incomprehensible to the likes of me. Weren't all whites omnipotent? What was she so scared of? What could I do to hurt her?

Mrs. Goldberg was as nondescript as her husband was striking. There was something grayish-pale bluish about her; mousy. She had deep-set large eyes, crowned with thick dark lashes, that seemed always to be painfully pondering weighty issues. Gray hair, with some traces of its former jet blackness in evidence, was pulled severely back and tied into a bun at the nape of the neck. Like hyphens, well manicured brows marked a wide forehead. The angular face was punctuated delicately with a carefully upturned nose and slightly generous mouth.

She walked with the scared stealth of a wary cat who has had too many close brushes with the tabby cat. Funny—not funny, ha! ha!, but funny in the disjointedness that made up her being. A rather large ungainly woman, she had a quiet, soft voice that was used very sparingly. When she gave an order, were it not for the steely unsmiling eyes, devoid of any expression, I'd have missed the unmistakable authority. Quietly insistent; never once did she raise her voice, yet she managed to convey a "you do as I say" manner without distasteful words such as duty, pay, passing through her lips.

Mr. Goldberg was in construction. Very good-looking, in a rugged, manly sort of way. Almost snow-white hair that seemed always in need of a cut contrasted well with the outdoor-man sinewy body that belied his age. Well over six foot, Mr. Goldberg moved with amazing swiftness and ease; graceful. This gentleman was a busy man around the house: he seemed never at a loss for a task to perform. However, he kept his zeal to himself. A big man gruff of voice, he was, nonetheless, gentle beneath it all.

After a very short while with this family, I came to feel somewhat sad, or intrigued rather, by the air of wariness that shrouded Mrs. Goldberg. Yes, intrigued rather than saddened, for she exuded the kind of quiet strength that made one aware of her being the solid rock on whom her entire family was anchored. Sad would be absurd . . .

Nonetheless, she was haunted, by God only knows what. I use the word haunted, for no other can portray the anxiety attacks that seemed to plague her each time she had to leave the house. Five times a week, because she worked Monday to Friday, half days, I would witness this odd behavior: before leaving, she would take leave of the whole house. Four bedrooms. A living-room. A dining-room. The kitchen. She all but took an inventory of the laundry, the pantry, and the garages and garden.

She would look at each room as if to keep a mental photograph of every article in every room and its relation to all the others in that room! It was as if she were arming herself to be able to spot any discrepancy, immediately upon return, should there be any, and she seemed in perpetual fear that there would be.

I had the feeling that if her whole house disappeared while she was away, she would not be altogether surprised; and, what is more, she would, at least, have the picture of the house within herself, a keepsake, a constant in a situation in which she felt threatened . . . with what obliteration?

Often I puzzled over what adventure or misadventure had rendered her thus suspicious, thus vulnerable, thus fearful. Had she once, long ago, come home to a horrendous scene of mass murder and looting? An empty house without man or matter? Or had some other disaster, a fire, a flood, or faulty structural component, a flaw in the building itself, perhaps, reduced house and all possessions to a pile of rubble. I wonder, now, could she have been seared by the Holocaust?

Jewish cooking is more savory than that of the English. It is also more sophisticated and elaborate than that of the Afrikaner. I was introduced to the separation of meat and milk; the rituals of Jewish life; the sabbath day off; matzo; and had a glimpse of the seriousness and purposefulness of the Jewish faith. A faith steeped in rich tradition. An exceedingly exclusive faith.

Houses are different from one another. They are different in shape, size, contents as well as, of course, the occupants they have. But the most significant yet subtle difference is the embodiment or soul of each house: the smell it exudes, has clinging to it as a stamp of character, like good perfume used by a woman who has come to know herself rather well.

The smells houses have come from the many activities and people in them — food, the washing, the preferred perfume of the lady of the house, the master's aftershave, and the facilities and time available to the maid are but a few. Though many of these are common to almost all houses, with the slightest variation, each house has its own blend. What is emphasized in one may be downplayed in another.

At the Goldbergs, fish and Frum vied for dominance. Those people certainly loved fish.

There were days when they had fish for breakfast, probably steamed, fried or poached; baked fish, of another kind, for lunch; and fried fish for dinner.

The house carried a fishy smell as a birthmark. However, scrupulous earnest cleanliness attempted to obliterate it from the air. Mrs. Goldberg didn't use ordinary soap in her kitchen. Part of her religion. Instead, a powder, Frum, would be placed on each dish, pot, spoon, or whatever was being washed in the kitchen sink. Minding not to mix milk dishes with meat dishes. The Frum would then be rubbed and spread on the article, and then rinsed off. This worked well if the dish hadn't been very greasy to start off with. Resolutely though, despite the Frum, fish grime and fish smell defied maid, madam, and religion at the Goldberg homestead.

From the other maids, I learnt that when there were house guests, it was custom to give the maid a little extra. So, I felt exploited at having to serve not only the couple who paid me but also the back-home-again not-long-married daughter and her son. However, when it became apparent, with time, that the expectant daughter-in-law was about to become my burden as well, bringing her washing and ironing, for me to do; eating, most nights, at her in-laws, my employers, I decided to bid this family adieu!

"Wanted, colored housemaid, cleaning, no cooking. R30 p.m. Apply Astoria Restaurant, Cape Town." Thus read the advertisement. Undeterred by not being colored, my dire financial need giving me unaccustomed courage and making me glib of tongue, eager to please, I applied for the job. The interview was deliberately impressive; Mr. Paporokoulus, the owner of the posh Astoria, interviewed me himself. A man of few words — English words — as I was to know later, he expressed his expectations in this simple manner – "No smoking, no drinking, no boyfriend. Polish floor, machine. Washing, machine. No cooking. *You,*" pointing significantly at my person, "eat food from the Astoria. Thirty rand a month," he added expansively. With an expressive shrug of shoulder — accompanied by spread hands, this tall, bony yet pleasing-looking gentleman, delivered his "who in her sane mind could refuse such?" offer. I accepted with alacrity, aware I was far from the only maid looking for a job. I would have accepted the job anyway; however, the obvious frills made it seem sent by heaven especially to me.

I was about to eat from the Astoria!

I who had glimpsed the wonder of the Astoria only because of its location in the center of Cape Town and right next to a bus stop. The sound of a band playing chintzy music, any day, any time, made this, yet another "whites-only" piece of South Africa, the more tantalizing, the more remote. And I was about to eat "from" the Astoria. At that point, the meaning of a plate of food, brought to me from a restaurant I could enter only as a maid who scrubbed and scoured somewhere in the bowels of the establishment far from the exclusive clientele who frequented it was completely lost to me. I was very glad to have that job, thrilled at the prospect of eating food from the Astoria. I felt I had reached the heights — eating food where I couldn't even be a waitress.

How soon our blessings pale when the drudgery of toil, sweat, and unrelieved long hours unmitigated by any appreciation, understanding or occasional word of kindness or praise begin to take its toll: Mrs. Paporokoulus, an immigrant like her husband, seemed to have chosen her new country because it answered a deep need within her being, struck a chord within her soul. She had heard that in South Africa the black people do not enjoy the protection of the law; that the workers, especially the domestic servants, were at the mercy of their employers. The usual adjunct that a white South African carries like a shield against accusations of racism, unfairness, and downright cruelty towards the indigenous people of that land — she had omitted to assimilate. Not for her the paternalistic "natives are childlike" attitude. She voiced no such, and, by action, displayed no such. She was bent on getting her money's worth from her servant, me. Mrs. Paporokoulus had golden looks. She had large eyes, that were luminous pools, widely set apart and fringed with long lashes the color of old gold. She had a curved body that reminded one of the statues for which her native land is famous: neatly pronounced calves tapered gently to well articulated ankles.

She had the enviable, awesome grace of the young lioness favored by the head of the pride.

Her voice, though, was jagged granite. She shrieked and shrieked when angry; which was very very often. Madam Paporokoulus had *airs*: "No, no, Sinya!" — she couldn't pronounce my name, the English name I used to go by then. "When picking phone you say Paporokoulus Reziidens!" she would screech, when I had answered the phone with "hello" or by rattling off the number.

The family was made up of two teenaged boys, belonging to Mrs. Paporokoulus from a previous marriage. From the same marriage had come the house the family now occupied in Milnerton. From the house next door, separated only by a low brick wall, had come Mr. P.

Their respective spouses, also Greek, had apparently fled back to Greece upon the breaking up of their marriages. Too hurt or too unworldly to think of teaming up, they had gone their separate ways, both to their motherland.

Here it was that I worked the hardest and longest hours. Mrs. Paporokoulus was not only a harsh medem, she was, by far, the most unreasonable and, I thought, least blessed with any intelligence.

A fleet of Greek cooks and Greek waiters occupied the servants' quarters of both houses. I was put in the small garage; the other big one housed the two cars and a van.

It wasn't long before this lady had contradicted her husband on virtually every clause of the verbal contract we had agreed upon: NO — she did not want me to use the polisher. "Girls" scratched the legs of the furniture by letting the polisher bump against them. I went on all fours using a hand-brush to polish her already shiny floors. NO — the laundry was to be done by hand. The new Bendix, according to her husband the best and most expensive washing-machine then available, was for her to use when between maids.

Yes, she wanted me in the kitchen at six o'clock so I could wake up the children at seven o'clock, at which time their freshly squeezed orange juice was to be ready, their lunches packed, their uniforms awaiting them in their dressing-rooms. Madam was not the least concerned that I, barely five or so years older than the children, had not left her kitchen the night before till the wee hours of the morning. The Astoria closed at midnight. As my food came with the Greek waiters who returned about 1 a.m. every night, that is when I had dinner. Also, my supper did not change for all the time I worked in this home. For years after I had left the employ of the Paporokouluses of the Astoria I could not eat curry. That is all the food I ever got out of the famous Astoria! Every night, for fifteen months. I lo-oo-ve curry, but . . .!

This early starting-time meant that, in fact, even on my days off, I couldn't spend the night at home. It was on one such night that I found myself in big bad trouble.

I had lingered longer than usual, reluctant to take leave of Thembeka, now two. By the time I finally tore myself away, it was past ten. Between waiting for the train at Nyanga station and unscheduled stops late-night trains seem to make as a matter of course, by the time I reached Cape Town station, the last bus to Milnerton had already left.

Slowly, as more trains from the back-of-beyond African townships disgorged themselves of their load, uncertain clumps began to form.

"The last Sea Point bus has left," said one bereft voice. Raised in lamentation, or hushed and fearful, strangers' voices joined in the dirge. Missed buses. No connection.

Soon some, finding their plight lightened by swelling numbers, chose to walk it. First, Green Point and Sea Point and surrounding areas grouped and departed. Before long there were enough mountain people — from Oranjezicht, Kloof Nek, and environs — to do likewise. But, I had left Oranjezicht. Milnerton lay in the opposite direction. Inaccessible.

Long after midnight I was alone at the bus stop where an hour or so before a group of despair-filled, cold and tired domestic servants had huddled. I stood alone. I did not know what to do or where to go. I faced deserted dark streets with forlorn lights spaced far apart and dimmed in their mournful isolation; threatened with things of the night. Unknown things. Wicked things. Dangerous and foreign things. Alone in a white town at night, I was frightened.

Then a man appeared from the shadows. When he came closer, I saw he was late forties, African, and had "village" written all over his face. Relief washed through me. The ability to take one look, sum up and categorize, was mine then. I had learnt black and white. And was far from knowledge of the very existence of gray, never mind shades thereof. Then, I was totally unaware of the complexity that human behavior is.

Tsotsis were town-bred and young. This man was neither. Therefore, I thought, he could not be dangerous. Luckily for me I was right. What is that famous saying about bliss and innocence of knowledge?

After he had told me who he was and from what part of the Transkei he hailed, and had listened to my plight, he offered me a place where I could spend the night.

Somewhere in Cape Town, midway between Green Point and the city center, in a compound, I spent the night with about a hundred men ranging in age from eighteen to sixty or so. My guardian angel commandeered a bed from a younger man who then went to share another. I spent the night there, and it was as if I was with my own brothers. My very own brothers.

Maids, new maids, get a lot of information about their madams. These are the people, same in rank, who have her employer's employment record: who has worked for her; what those maids have said about her; how they left and why; how much she paid them; what quirks, weaknesses, likes and dislikes she has. Has she some redeeming characteristic. If so, what is it?

Unfortunately, all this information, valuable as it is, is of little use to the maid, in the actual selection process. She has no way of using it, as a way of choosing whether or not to work for this particular white woman. It is information she gets, can only get, in most instances, after she is indeed working for her.

However, this is not to say this information is not useful to the maid. She can still use it in determining whether or not she will move her belongings here from the other maids' rooms, her erstwhile neighbors. Maids move in completely only after several months, when they've figured out they are staying.

Mrs. P was well known, among the maids in Milnerton, for the ridiculously long hours she worked her maids.

Mrs. Paporokoulus, like all the women I have worked for as a domestic servant, never once heard how I sounded when annoyed. That doesn't mean I never was annoyed. To the contrary, I was so much and so often annoyed that had I opened my mouth, I doubt I'd have lasted a week in any of these jobs. But I chose never to sink so low that I'd engage in a screaming match with these women.

"She probably doesn't even have JC," I'd think, saying nothing, so angry I'd sometimes almost feel her neck in my slowly squeezing hands. "I will not be a fishmonger's wife." Haughtily, I let the madams insult me, since, it seemed, that was part of what they expected for the miserable pittance I received at their hands.

When I had had enough, I packed my bags, went to the madam and told her, "I'm leaving." That never failed to astound them. Because I'd fought to say not a word in argument, defense or attack, these women had believed I was happy at their insults.

There is a generally held myth that the verbal contract between maids and madams is binding. Since the contract both assumes and confirms the infallibility of madams, it binds only the maid. If a madam feels like sacking her "girl" without the benefit of a month's notice she can do so: as long as, in her eyes, the girl did something wrong.

Wrong things, in white women's eyes, are stealing, the synonym for misplaced (as I don't know where I put it); missing (as taken by another member of the family); drunk, which could be anything from "had a glass or two" to "can hardly stand on own two legs"; rowdy, broadly speaking, this has happened whenever two friends or more dropped by; and a host of similar evils. Most improbable, for the maid, not to err. The maid is accused of such or worse for, otherwise, the madam owes her a month's wages for dismissing her without cause.

The maid, on the other hand, has no way of extracting that amount when she feels like quitting because she has been wronged. That is what happened when I quit working for Mrs. Paporokoulus. She refused to give me my money and I went to the police station.

The police were unable to help me, for this lady had not bothered to register me with the Bantu Administration as her maid. In the eyes of the police, I was not working for Mrs. Paporokoulus of Milnerton.

"When you want to leave the woman, pack your bags. In fact, from the beginning of the month, start taking your things, one by one, away. On the last day of the month, she gives you your money and you say, 'Thank you, Medem,' walk out of her kitchen and close the door. Wait a little bit in your room. Then leave as if you are going to the shop or visiting another 'girl.'"

"Since these women always pay us at night, and since you have nothing now in your room, just walk out. Like that."

Such pearls of domestic-work wisdom, I had not yet heard. Others, who had lived this work experience for decades knew better how to endure it. Not me. Not then.

From this family, newly immigrated to South Africa, I inherited resentment. Resentment that white anyone from anywhere in the world can come to South Africa and be what I could never be. Do what I could never do. Enjoy luxury I could not even dream of.

Years later at South Africa House in London, I was flabbergasted to learn the conditions, extremely enticing, under which people such as the Paporokoulus family came to South Africa. The white government of my country, a government that has every conceivable argument to support denying me bread, roof, work, happiness, and the right to call myself a citizen of the country of my birth, blithely, without qualms or twinge of conscience, invites, sponsors, and welcomes foreigners to take what is denied me. This same government lavishes on these transplanted whites (for that is the only criterion for the invitation) even the political rights it has systematically taken away from me and mine, over the centuries.

Of all the members of the oppressing class in South Africa, it is, for me, this group that chooses to become my exploiters, my oppressors, the rapists of my pride and violators of my humanhood, that I find hardest to swallow.

A hard finishing-school

After the Paporokoulus Residence experience, Guguletu seemed a haven. Having to leave "the kitchen" well after one in the morning, more than all other liberties this woman took with me, more than all the other abuses put together, showed me the cruel power white women can, if they allow themselves, wield over their darker sisters.

I was no stranger to hard work. My own mother, sometimes father too, would raise a child from deepest sleep, any hour of the night, to do a job left undone or to finish one half-done. But that was punishment. I was supposed to be a worker, an employee, not a sinner serving penance, at the "reziidens" of this self-proclaimed Greek goddess. I opted for sleep-out jobs.

There were tremendous advantages, I now thought, to a sleep-out job. I would be able to see more of my child. And be more readily available if a teaching position became vacant. What, compared to these, were those supposed advantages of sleep-in jobs? The meals? Most employers have no qualms about giving their maids different fare from their own. Although I have never seen this in Cape Town, butchers in other centers of South Africa proudly display signs advertising "boys' meat." Furthermore, as the Paporokoulus job had shown me, I couldn't bank on getting more sleep just because I spent my nights where I worked.

An additional attraction was that sleep-out jobs were reputed to pay more. And that I believe. Since the maid doesn't eat all her meals there, pays rent in the township, and has traveling costs to bear, employers tend to give them more of what is due to all domestic servants. No domestic servant is paid enough. Moreover, those madams whose servants sleep in actually deduct unknown and unnegotiated amounts from the wages of the domestic servants, without taking into account their other commitments to their own households. Since the latter doesn't know, hasn't been told, exactly how much she is underpaid, "because she gets free meals here" or "she has a room and I buy the uniform she wears," she can complain neither about the food nor about the accommodation she indirectly pays for.

This is not to say domestic servants are too dumb to understand their exploitation. No, Siree. Neither am I saying domestic servants are candidates for canonization. They are as human as the medems. I know, not only because I was a domestic servant; but because, each morning and each evening I worked "sleep-out," I learned from the experts.

During those trips to and from work, in the dying tradition of my people, tales were told by brilliant storytellers — weary women, who get up in the mornings long before the milkman's piercing pre-dawn whistle, prepare husbands, prepare children of school-going age, prepare little ones, to be taken wherever they will be cared for. They prepare each member of the family for his or her day. The domestic servant then prepares herself and leaves to face her own day.

Evenings, after a full day's work and much more, she returns to hem her family's day, for without her loving hand's toil, it would come undone.

What I heard, on the buses to and from the black townships — where one hears and one learns — is as valid as any data based on scientific probings; only, much more exciting, much more alive!

An old woman, a veteran domestic servant, says, "My sisters, that old stingy so-and-so I work for gives me things I wouldn't even take to the church rummage sale. But me, I know what these white women we work for think of us. I know how they think. If I don't take her rags she will hate me. So, I take the rags, my sisters, let her wrap them and make a nice parcel. When she gives me a parcel she also gives me a ride to the bus terminus. Hey, this saves me bus fare and my tired leg-bones. Me, I am old. If the rags will give me a ride, I say thank you to the rags. Ha, ha, ha! When she puts me off the car in Claremont, me ha-ha ... I take the rags and put them in the nearest dustbin I can find, right there at the station, and then take my bus home."

Another woman chirps in, "Wethu, you must always take anything she gives you. One day she may even give you something you will be able to use. Encourage her!" Talk about interdependence: in giving rags the lady gives hope.

The configurations vary, but the basic ingredients are the same: on bus or train, the passengers traveling daily on the same route begin to group themselves. In these informal structures the domestic workers air their grievances, share strategies, joke about a starkly harsh and brutal work environment, and console one another; thus fortified, they advance to tackle their individual loads.

On the trip home, the same thing happens but probably in different groups. The frustrations of that particular day or of another, long gone, are thrown to the group to examine, compare, ridicule, and reduce to the absurdity that they are. The domestic worker returns to her community and her family healed and restored.

The bus journey (for these women) taking them to and from work also takes them away from and back to the tenuous security of their lives. It is a journey that jettisons them, daily, into the soul-battering, itself soulless world of white madams who employ them. Therefore, for the domestic workers, the bus journey is both deliverance from dire poverty and a delivering into the very hell that makes the difference between having no money and having very little money. They are not slaves. They are frighteningly close, though.

It is here that I learnt of the games madams play.

"If you are new and you find money under one of the beds, turn it in, at once! Those people can even collect dust and put it on a coin or a note to make it look like it has been there for a long time. That money is a trap to see if you're a thief."

"Oh, and don't ever let them catch you eating from their plates or using their cups. They can kill you for that. You know, *abelungu* (white people) are funny people. They'll let dogs lick their plates before they can allow a black person to eat from those same plates!"

"I hear they sleep with dogs!"

"Awu! I don't know about that. How could one sleep with a dog? But, of course, we all know they kiss them! Haa-ha-ha! Oh, really, *abelungu* are other people. No, they are not at all like us!"

"Me, a cow would first bear a human baby and horses grow horns before I will kiss a dog!"

"Yhuu! And as for the one (madam) I work for now. Yhoo! I feel so sorry for the *arme* (poor) husband of hers. You know this woman leaves the house just after the husband goes out to work. EVERY DAY! When on a shu-shu day, she is in the house, she is married to that phone. You know who she is talking to? That 'doctor' of hers who never comes to see her when master is around! They think I am a child, those two. Aargh! Shame, and master is soo-o-o nice. *Hayi* (oh, no), that woman, she is another woman! She has no heart at all for master!"

"Yhuu! Women, listen to this one! Do you think she is right here upstairs (pointing to her head)? Is this woman worrying herself about the games *abelungu* women play on their husbands? You know, my sister, you have time to waste. If you are not careful, you will lose your job.

"*Abelungu* pay you to worry about their dirt, that's all. Finish and *klaar*! Me, you will never find me worrying about the problems of *abelungu*.

"That is why you mustn't listen to her when she starts her '*Nyeh-nyeh-nyeh*' business. They like to tell you all their secrets. '*Nyeh-nyeh-nyeh*' — you have to listen to her complaints about her husband who works too hard and is never home. '*Nyeh-nyeh-nyeh*!' Her mother-in-law doesn't like her. '*Nyeh-nyeh-nyeh*!' Now her mother is changing her will and she will not get all the money. Her no-good sister will get some.

"Me! As soon as she starts, I just say, 'Yes, medem . . . yes medem . . . mmmh! Oh, ag shame, medem' — I don't even look at her. All the time she's going '*Nyeh-nyeh-nyeh*' I go on with my work.

"That woman! If I stopped to listen to her endless complaints about everybody I would never finish my work. And then, when I want to go to my other chars, she starts pleating her brow, closes her eyes to slits, forgets she has wasted my time.

"But I learned after some time. I go on working. Now she thinks I'm dumb. But I'm not interested in her silly stories. I have no time for white women's gossip or their stupid problems.

"Those people have so much money and so much time, they go out and buy problems! My medem started *jolling* (having a lover) after that water-head husband of hers bought her another house. This big house in Newlands was not enough? No! He had to go and buy a house in Gordon's Bay! My dear, when she goes there, I can't even take my day off. I must look after master. You know what that means? If he leaves the house, I must call her at once! Of course, water-head doesn't know that."

"But really, can you people tell me what it is these white women want? They have big beautiful houses, cars, money, clothes, food that could feed Hitler's army, they don't have to work, not even in their own houses. What do they want? What are they looking for? I wish I could be in their place."

"Oh, I don't want to be in their place. The day I would let another person touch my underwear, any time of the month, whhosh . . . I would know my heart was dead! What women are these who have nothing private?"

"Mine! Mine walks alone (*Uhamba yedwa*). None is like her, I swear! Where have you seen a white woman who wants me to patch her children's clothes? Me, patch? Oh, I told her. From then on, she never worried me with her nonsense of patching. Me, I fixed her! These people, you must not put them in your pocket. They will tear it. From the start, tell them what's what!"

"Hey, let me tell you about *my* medem! I laugh at that one. Me and she, we are the same age. She is walking with a walking-stick, but she will be saying, to me, 'Mary, run, get the phone. Mary, tonight I am having ten people to dinner. What do you think we should give them? Mary, the laundry! Mary, the ironing!' All the time she sits and sits and only her mouth is working. 'Mary. Mary. Mary!' I tell you, that one will be dying but she will still be telling me what to do! And do you know what? We were expecting our first babies together, at the same time. Now her third, her youngest, is a doctor at Groote Schuur Hospital. Do you want to know how much she pays me, this woman, after all these years? Thirty rands! Thirty rands, I tell you, after they have killed me with their work. *Abelungu!* Those are not people. They laugh with you, while, at the same time, they kill you. Me, I will never forget them, *abelungu!*"

"Mine is Black Sash, The Girls (*Amantombazana*), you know. People (blacks) are always knocking at the door coming with their problems. Shame, medem is kind to them and she helps everybody. She is always saying the government is wrong. She pays me better. She gives me money for the books of the children. She takes my girls to town and buys them clothes for Christmas . . ."

"*You*, are so lucky!"

"My friend, you do not know the children of today if you say so. You should hear my daughters! 'What does this white woman want from us? Who told her we want things chosen for us by a white woman? You know mama, white women don't know anything about clothes. They have no taste!' And the other one will add, 'They have no style and they think we're stupid. How can that old woman know anything about the clothes of young people? And, the shop she takes us to — WOOLWORTHS! Yhuu! You, mama, and your medem make me laugh!' Those are my daughters' words. I send those clothes home to the village. The people there are not fussy, my friends. They are naked."

"*Heyi*! Let me tell you . . . you don't know nothing about *abelungu*. Ask me. When I was a little girl we were living on the farms. My grandmother told me about things that happened when she was little. *Abelungu! Abelungu* have no hearts. No hearts at all: Do you know, if a sheep was lost and they thought maybe one of the 'boys,' as they call our men, if they thought one of the boys had stolen it they sjambokked him until he died?"

"Kill a man for a sheep! Heh-h?"

"What are you asking this woman? What are you asking? Even today, how many hearts are you seeing taken out of white dying people and given to us? When? Don't white people die? Aren't they taking our hearts and giving them to other *abelungu*, hey?"

"Wethu, let me finish the thing I was telling you. Do you hear me? Don't think after they had killed the man that was the end of the story; oh no! They had to show the other kaffirs what's what."

"So, what did they do?"

"Women, these people would throw the body in those big *oonds* (ovens) made from oil drums and let him roast there in it. When he was just bones, pure white bones, you know, they would gather there and open the door of the *oond* for all to see. It was a big joke for them because the man no longer had lips or anything, his teeth were showing, and the *abelungu* would say to each other, pointing to the bones, '*Kyk, die kaffir lag!*' ('Look, the kaffir laughs.')"

Another bus, another day, a different hour, a different group, the interaction might be the same or quite different. Some groups become hymn- and prayer-oriented; others focus on family-related issues; and others still, perhaps, on "what is becoming of the world" — the world constituting the changing mores of the rigidly controlled society. There are groups who are into money consolidation schemes, adult education, and many more. Sometimes a group will become an *ad hoc* group when a special need arises, as when a member dies or loses someone in her family. Then the bus group or the train group will collect money among the members and come and be with the family of their traveling friend during the crisis.

"My sister, 'we' are moving," a woman will announce to her companions one day. "So I will be changing to another bus."

On her last day with her group, she brings something to share with them: a packet of sweets, scones, a prayer, or some other. She is given something one of the group made or bought and for which the group will reimburse her later.

I was struck by the wholeness of women who, I knew, would be transformed, the minute they opened the gates of the houses where they toiled. From the alert, vivacious, knowledgeable, interesting people they were on these buses, they would change to mute, zombie-like figures who did not dare have an idea, opinion, or independent thought about anything, anything at all. Not even what color they would look best in!

The madam of the house makes the decision about the interior decor. Her likes determine, therefore, what color overalls shall be donned by the maid. Yes, she who will never, not once, be in those overalls, chooses what color they will be. But, on the other hand, since the overalls could conceivably last longer than a maid, perhaps it is just as well the madam buys them in the color she prefers.

For me, domestic service was a real expansion exercise in that, for the first time, I lived among white people — people I had, up to this time, seen and experienced only as priests, doctors, invisible owners of those big shops in town, police, Bantu inspectors, administrators, superintendents and government. That white people were *all*-powerful, all wealthy beyond measure, happy, clean, well dressed, these last two often serving as synonyms in my mind, and employed people like us, I had always vaguely known. What I had not known was that their perception of people like us did not quite coincide with our perception of who we were and what we were about.

More than anything, however, being a domestic servant did more to me than it did for me. It introduced me to the fundamentals of racism.

Remember, now, I am not ungrateful. Those four years in the white homesteads did benefit me greatly. Am I not alive? Are my children not alive? I did earn enough to keep body and soul together; but at what cost! Each morning as I prepared and served breakfast, made school lunches, dressed kids for school, walked kids to same, in my body beat the heart of a mother whose own were left untended. Many a time, I recall, did I see myself as the mother wolf who had had to leave her cubs with a jackal to go and search for food during a particularly long and hard-hitting drought. The tale ends with the mother wolf having succeeded only in having her children eaten by the jackal. My very endeavors to maintain my family contained the seeds for its destruction. Later, I was to learn of the white South African woman's anguish upon becoming a working mother. Mine was not the choice of being a working mother or a not-working mother. No. I could choose between being a working mother or having no children left. Whose mother would I have been had my children died from starvation? The money I earned was the only money we had to live on. If I hadn't gone out to work, there would be no three children to talk about. They did not have a lot of things. They had no dolls, no clothes, except what we bought from rummage sales, hand-medowns that had been handed down. They had no nutritious food, never mind anything plentiful or delicious. They had no bedtime stories, no books. No day-care centers and no pre-schools to go to: had these been available, I could not have afforded them.

From the very beginning, I had little support from my husband in supporting the child. A laborer, he did not earn much. But even had that not been the case I doubt I would have seen much of his money. My husband was stingy.

2

More than two years had passed since my fall from grace. Life was a humdrum existence, sweaty for the most part, with a rather bleak prognosis. Timid attempts, on my part, at getting a teaching position had not been rewarded. My letters to the Secretary of the School Board did not even elicit a reply.

Twice, my former principal walked all the way from Nyanga to Guguletu, to my parents' house where I had lived when I was a member of his staff. The first time he had found my mother despite the fact that my parents had moved from NY 12 to NY 74. Mr. Mokhachane had a vacancy at his school both times he came for me. He wanted me back.

The School Board, unfortunately, did not share his enthusiasm. He never got me back. My sad loss.

The second time he came I was home. "Mistress," he said, "what happened the last time?" I told him I had gone to the Secretary of the School Board as he had instructed me. I had gone there taking the forms he had left me, having first completed them.

"Thank you, mistress." I couldn't fault him. The Secretary of the School Board had been courteous as he received those forms from my hands. When you offer something to an older person or to one of much higher rank, in my culture, you use both of your hands. A sign of respect. My mother brought me up properly. And I badly needed that post. "You'll be hearing from us, mistress," the Secretary had said, dismissing me with what, like a traveler in the desert convinces himself that shimmer yonder is an oasis, I took for a smile.

This time, Mr. Mokhachane was taking no chances. He helped me complete the forms. But even with such help, I did not succeed in returning to Hlengisa Higher Primary School. To this day, I have no idea why I was so unlucky in this respect.

"Mistress, are you sure you never crossed him or quarreled with him?" asked another school principal who, twice before, had tried to get me to come and teach at his school. Our combined efforts had, twice, failed. Now, this gentleman had come to try, once more, to have me on his staff.

Mr. Malunga just couldn't understand my luck. I could not help him any. I couldn't understand it myself. No bribe, cash or kind, had ever been, even by a roundabout way, alluded to. The possibility does exist, of course, that the hint (if hint there was) was so subtle it went right over my head.

Still ringless, still working as a domestic servant, I was again pregnant. Feeling betrayed by the world at large but especially by a body that refused to wait for ring or lobola (Luthando was nowhere near achieving this goal) I decided two children were as good as any reason to go through a civil ceremony. Getting parental consent would not be easy. We did without.

The Native or Bantu Commissioner, himself neither native nor Bantu, perfunctorily went through the brief ceremony, one or two of the clerks serving as witnesses. Inside five or ten minutes, the whole thing was over.

As we left the forbidding building called Standard House the fear that always grips me when I am in government offices fell away. Now, vague amazement at how easy it had been to effect such a radical transformation filled me. Not quite filled me: there was more than a tinge of disquiet in what I was feeling. Disquiet and some disappointment. Never had I imagined my wedding so lonely!

The weddings of my childhood were community celebrations: ululating women paved the way, spreading their shawls on the ground, before the bride and groom as they stepped out of church buildings. Bodies, so many the shack church was blocked from view by the sheer numbers of the joyous throng.

Wide, smiling, sun-kissed skies looked down on the dancers: men leaping, prancing, gyrating to the loud, hot clappings of maidens whose full throats sent out song melodious enough to move bones in ancestral graves. Trembling, agitating shoulders also answered the call of song; rhythmically, in unison, shoulders moved in a poem of motion.

Wedding cakes, wedding bread, meat, beer, and stacks of other food besides. A feast. Weddings were feasts when I was growing up.

The bride, covered in lace from head to toe, this one day to look the most beautiful for all to see. This is the day she steps not on soil, floating on the congratulations of old and young. Black-suited groom, in gloves, walks beside his pure-white-lace-clad bride. Arms, locked; perfect match. She, with eyes downcast, displays to all the fearful knowledge that is hers. She is leaving the only home she has ever known, for the word of the man who has said it is she he will cherish till he draws the last of his given breath. He walks her as if she were some fragile petal from a rare exotic flower.

Ceremonies were conducted at the home of the bride, at church, and finally, at the groom's home where the whole wedding party eventually ends up. Her people accompany her to her new home and leave her behind, leave her crying because the words they leave behind are a raw reminder of life's many tortuous twists.

Besides the negotiations and planning, the actual wedding takes a whole weekend. That is the kind of wedding I knew as a child.

That is the wedding picture that was planted in my mind. Weddings touched and transformed whole communities. And long after the day, people still talked about so-and-so's wedding, the bride's dresses, for after the actual ceremony she changed for tea, changed for a walk and changed for this and for that. Two or three changes. So did the bridesmaids and the groom.

And the two families whose children had joined as one had a new way of addressing each other: "Mkhozi" — one of the most respect-filled terms one is ever likely to find in the Xhosa language. It is a term used by the people of one side of a union to those of the other, a reminder of the relationship that, no matter what, can never again be as if it had not been: children will be born, perpetuating the relationship beyond this present; beyond that which we, *"mkhozi,"* can now see.

Except for the small gold-colored band on my ring finger, nothing was new.

My parents were furious. When the reasons behind the act became known, mother sobbed, "After you said you were sorry, ooh, a person! It is very hard to put one's trust in a person." Clearly, I had let her down, horribly, and left her sitting on a hard place. Father's reaction was the harder to bear: he maintained a stony silence, retreated into himself, and went about as if all should know he had said, "Her name shall not be said in this house."

The civil ceremony effectively removed father's authority over me, transferring that honor to my husband. And it was not long before I knew the difference.

Throughout what turned out to be a short, if fecund, marriage we never had a house we called ours or home. We did not qualify to rent a council house. At first, we had not even bothered to go to the administration office to apply for a house. As we were not legally married, we did not qualify for permission to rent a house.

When we were married, we did not go because we knew of couples who had been on the waiting-list for donkey's years. It just didn't make sense, losing a day at work chasing the shadow of a dream.

Shacks abound in the African townships. The housing shortage there is a well-known fact. People in the townships have reacted in various creative ways to this stressful situation, and building shacks in the back yards is but one. It is in one such shack that we lived.

I was still working in white people's homes, doing sleep-out jobs. My husband's job had taken him away from Cape Town to one of the little towns in the Karoo. His visits were a rarity; not that I was complaining. The glamor of marriage and the heat of desire were thinning faster than a dog with mange loses his hair.

Now, with Luthando away, I moved back to my parents' home. A typical Guguletu four-roomed house. No extension. Mother and father. Their seven children, and now, my Thembeka.

A year earlier, Jongi had married Priscilla Nonkululeko Xelisilo, a woman of the Gxarha clan. She had been given the married first name (*igama lomzi*) of Nolusapho, Mother of family, for, as the wife of the eldest son, she would be expected to give a home to any of our extended family who, for one reason or another, became in need of one. Six months before my second child was born, Jongi and Nolusapho were blessed with the birth of their daughter, Elphina Nomfundo. Therefore, when in due time, I had Thokozile Fezeka, thirteen souls breathed under the roof of NY 74 no. 33. Thirteen, in a house where, under normal circumstances, no more than three people should live. Four, at most, and if you want to stretch it. And if the couple's two children are of the same sex. Four. Absolute maximum. Obviously, we had long exceeded that maximum. And we were far from being the largest family in Guguletu.

If Luthando's visits were infrequent, what was even less frequent, and more bothersome, were his remittances. I saw very little of his money. And he didn't have much to start off with.

Since I had not planned on making childbearing a career, I had not thought it necessary to horde Thembeka's baby-clothes. Need is always great in the townships. And I doubt that there exists in this world a more heart-strings-pulling need than the need of an infant.

Thembeka, although I did not think so at the time, was to be the most fortunate of my three babies as far as her layette was concerned. I was teaching when I expected her. Luthando had not yet discovered absolute power. And she was the first baby and first real responsibility we had.

My second pregnancy found me an established domestic servant: I had been through three medems in sleep-in jobs, two in sleep-out jobs, and was now doing chars; here today, there tomorrow, and, God knows who, among the white women who see you once a week, thinks you are *her* employee and would be there for you if you needed her. Char work seems to me the least secure job in a class of jobs where security is scarce indeed.

Where I had actually knitted pretty little frilly things for Thembeka, the second pregnancy found me scrounging around for cast-offs. I had very little money in spite of being employed. I wasn't wasting it on silks and furs either. I do not drink. I do not smoke. I did not know the color of caviar. T-bone steak, the name, I did not even know.

I toiled dutifully and uncomplainingly. And, I hoped! I had not given up on myself. I applied to training hospitals. Nursing and teaching were the only professions known to people like me. Outright rejections were few. Mostly, the hospitals either didn't bother replying or one was put on a waiting-list longer than an elephant's memory. Then, a hospital in Durban admitted me. I was to begin training February 1.

The year was 1965. There was the little snag of my second pregnancy.

I wrote telling the hospital I was under obligation and on contract until the end of June. Luck was with me. "Then come for the 1st of July," replied the hospital.

Mother, dear soul, was prepared to saddle herself with a two-month-old baby as well as Thembeka, then almost two and a half. "A saint," I thought, "and after what I have done."

Before we were married, I had indicated this intention to my husband. He had watched me write letters of application, complete forms and wait, and wait, agonizing with each week's passing. Now preparations were afoot: buy a watch with a second hand. Get duty shoes; special scissors; and a host of other items besides.

With absolutely no support from my husband, with some from mother, who was beside herself, I managed to get everything on the list the hospital had sent me. Father's battered suitcase would have to do.

Thokozile was due in April. I had two months to go. This time, I vowed, I would work hard and not look back. One good thing about being a trainee nurse, I would get only five rand less than the teacher's salary I would have been earning.

"I cannot have my wife hundreds of miles away in Durban while I am in Cape Town," declared my husband. We both knew that I was the one who supported the children; that this training was the best hope for our future well-being. Purgatory unannounced opened up and swallowed me whole. The legal status of African women in South Africa gave husbands such authority that defying my husband would have been more stupid than his injunction. I have never hated anyone more than I hated Luthando at that time. But I hated myself even more. I could not believe I had, with no coercion from anybody, while of sane mind, voluntarily, nay, eagerly, placed myself in the custody of such a man. I had chosen him: and with both my eyes wide open!

Where I had seen a friend and a lover, stood an adversary and a rapist. The man on whom I had planned to lean became the cruel current sweeping away the seeds of hope, a nightmare squashing and crushing my dreams.

Materially, my parents had not been able to give me much. But, thank God, they had instilled in me unshakeable belief in myself and in my capabilities. Moreover, I had not in my home witnessed irresponsibility. I did not have that way out in my bag of tricks. To me, people grew up to do their duty. Mine was clearly hauling myself back to the state of professional respectability. And I took the first step: I ceased caring for my husband. He no longer was in my heart.

I worked until the morning, in my ninth month, that I woke up with the now-remembered heaviness, the hint of my period coming. I sent for the ambulance. Experience is the best teacher: when I arrived at the Somerset Hospital, this time, I expected to deliver by Caesarean section. Now I knew medical terms like "disproportion."

Waking up and seeing my daughter for the first time, I was not filled with dread and doubts as to her authenticity. Unlike the first time, I knew the closed eyes would open, the folds around the neck would disappear, the tiny fists would unfold and straighten to normal-fingered hands. And, there might even come to be some physical aspects in this stranger that I would recognize.

I returned home to swell the number by one more.

Not long after Thokozile and I returned from the hospital, we were alone in the house because everyone had gone to church:

"Come in," I shouted, answering someone's "*Nkqo! Ngqo!*" — the onomatopoeic knock of the Xhosa people.

"*UnguSindiwe?*" ("Are you Sindiwe?") the tall, strapping stranger asked. I nodded, taken by surprise both by the wonder in her voice as well as the question itself. I was certain I had never seen the woman who stood at the doorway, filling it and completely blocking out the sunlight that was the only relief to the gloom our house wore like a badge.

"Sindiwe, *uyandazi?*" ("Sindiwe, do you know me?")

"*Hayi*" ("No"), I replied, for that was the truth. I did not know her.

"*Mntakabhuti! Mntakabhuti!*" And with that ("Brother's child! Brother's child!"), tears started down her cheeks.

By this time I had slid off the bed where I'd been nursing Thoko. Simultaneously, we approached each other. Now, we were hugging, wet cheeks rubbing, as we kissed. Then, back we stood, holding each other at arms length the better to survey each other; and again clasped each other, embracing.

That is how, on a Sunday morning, I met my Aunt Dathini for the first time in twenty years. I was twenty-two. She was about mother's age or a few years younger.

I made tea while she crooned over the baby. My parents had not bothered with announcements this time, so she had not heard I was expecting another child. Neither had she heard about my marriage. For the same reason.

I soon found out, my Aunt Dathini was not one to beat about the bush. Questions came chasing each other: "What does this husband of yours do?" Ooh! Educated as I was, why had I married a nobody, a nothing of a laborer. "Haven't you cheated yourself, *Mntakabhuti*?"

When she heard I'd had an operation, Aunt Dathini demanded the baby's napkins so she could wash them. What had I planned to feed those who had gone to church? Was there a child, nearby, we could send to the shops? She had brought some vegetables with her but now she thought it would not be a bad idea if she added a little more meat to what we had.

By the time the rest of the family returned, Aunt Dathini and I were chatting away as if we had grown up playing *"upuca"* (five stones) together. She had a knack, I was to learn later, of making barriers disappear; for she had never learnt the meaning of inhibition. And to each moment, she gave her zestful attention.

This half-sister of my father's is beautiful. Taut, dark, flawless skin reveals gracious, regal features. Dathini, in her youth, could have graced the covers of international fashion magazines. Her body, even beneath folds of cheap wear that would camouflage, is a work of art. No sculptor could have done better. Her eyes can be whirlpools of venomous fires when provoked. Ordinarily though, they are twin depths of mirth — alert and full of *joie de vivre*. But it is her voice that forces you to catch your breath. A natural orator, Dathini has a voice to match. Singing, she rivals the famous Miriam Makeba.

That first Sunday, however, when father asked: *"Ngubani na lo?"* ("And who may this be?") — asking standing just inside the door, not even taking his hat off or putting his briefcase down — the voice could only manage an emotion-chocked whisper: *"Bhuti!"*

The look of utter surprise-kissed joy on father's usually expressionless face was something to behold. A tumultuous reunion between Aunt Dathini and my parents followed. For as soon as Aunt Dathini had said "*Bhuti*," father had replied, "Dathini!" — the years falling away, dissolving right before us all.

Then each child was introduced, because except for Jongi and me, and, of course, our late sister Siziwe, Anti had seen none of her other nephews and nieces. The first three of us were village born. Dathini and mother had missed each other on the mercifully few times mother had gone back with one or two of the little ones to the village, always on some sad family business; for Aunti Dathini had worked for years in East London.

Dad'oBawo (aunt on father's side) may have come late into my life, but of my blood relatives she is the one I know the most. I know more of her than I know of my mother for she has shown me so much of herself.

"Sindi, Brother's child, you have to remember that *ndibomvu*" (that is, "I am red, unschooled"). She said that often. To get sympathy or to con me into doing something for her. As I grew to know her and her ways, I got to know that she was a woman of formidable talents.

Talents, she had needed in abundance. Those she had not been naturally endowed with, she appropriated with ease, good sense helping her to make wise decisions.

Her latest decision was to come to Cape Town, after spending more than ten years in East London. She told us: "I heard the Cape Town medems paid a whole lot better."

Dathini had been in Cape Town for six months before she was able to track us down. Long ago, my parents had tried to keep links with their relatives in the village. But we are not a writing people, culturally. And this cultural trait is very strong in my family. The last Dathini had heard of her half-brother's family was when we were living in Retreat.

Retreat was, by the time she came to Cape Town, a colored residential area. Africans had been moved to Nyanga and Guguletu. She had asked about us; and kept on asking until one lead led to another. And, eventually, she had come knocking at our door that Sunday morning.

Aunt Dathini was working on the farms of Philippi that border Guguletu on the north. Her nails were cracked and blackened. She was burnt several shades darker than her natural coffee color. Her tall frame stooped a little, trained by long hours bent over endless rows of cabbages. Weeding. By hand.

Dad'oBawo was to be instrumental in my getting a job later on. A few weeks after she found us, she found herself a better job. As a domestic servant in a small white suburb that had, and, two decades later, still has, "emerging poor-white" written on each door of each pretentious little house there.

Ottery is a white suburb in the doldrums of the Cape Flats. Far from the city. Far from the real farming area. Its residents have that indecisive look of South African whites who have left the Platteland behind but are still not quite at home in the city. Caught in the twilight zone, neither here nor there.

Dathini had not been working there a month when a white woman who met her at the local café asked her whether she knew of anyone who wanted work. She knew me.

Ottery's proximity to Guguletu made the job very appealing. So did the fact that Aunt Dathini was there.

Mr. and Mrs. Koorn were Afrikaners. They were probably about thirty years of age and had two children, a girl aged about ten and a boy, a brat who must have been six or seven. They were definitely not rich. Both husband and wife had to work; they lived in a municipal house in a working-class neighborhood; had one car.

My monthly salary was generous at thirty rand a month — when I eventually went back to a teaching job, my salary was less than five rand above this.

The work was far from back-breaking. Mrs. Koorn wanted to come home to a beds-made, floors-swept, rugs-vacuumed, bathrooms-tidied, and a meal-ready-to-serve house. She put the family wash in the washing machine at weekends and I did the ironing during the week. I did learn to cook some savory dishes, though.

The saying amongst domestic workers on this matter is that the Afrikaners cook or enjoy tasty food whilst the English boil everything to death with a sprinkling of salt and a dash of pepper.

More than any other of the families I have worked for or, later, known under a different set of circumstances, the Koorns were instrumental in my belated socialization regarding color of skin as determinant of social status in South Africa. The only reason I worked for them and not they for me, was that I was black and they were white. They were less educated than I was even then. They, like me, had not been born into money. They had won no grand prize. In fact, when I worked for them, they had little beside what they brought home come pay day. Granted, I had fallen on hard times. Had our positions been reversed, though, could the same have happened, in reverse? Having fallen on very hard times, could the Koorns have ended up working for me, if I had the money to employ them? NO! The law forbids it. What is more, the law has ensured that it can never be.

You see, the Koorns are eligible for welfare. I am not. The Koorns are eligible for decent remuneration. I am not.

A white South African, given government support from cradle to grave, has to work hard to be poor. Poor is the "natural" status of working blacks in South Africa. Give me any criterion for poverty and, I dare say, at least seventy-five per cent or more of the Africans in full employment qualify with flying colors.

Unassuming and exhibiting no malice towards me, long having accepted the order of things, comfortable and unquestioning, these people are the backbone of Afrikaner power. The well-meaning, unthinking sheep who will forever follow the leader. Naive, and dangerous by virtue of that same fact, they, totally uncomprehending, choose the people who run the country.

Mrs. Koorn, plumpish, of medium height, conscientiously cultivated a city look. She went to tremendous pains, alas unsuccessful, to disguise the strong strain of farmers' stock from whence she came. If she had a fault, it would be that she, perhaps because of her youth, had not quite made up her mind regarding the kind of relationship she would have with her maid. Almost girlishly confiding one day, she would, upon recalling our respective stations in life, vigorously attempt to reclaim lost ground, perhaps reminding herself more than me (for I never did forget it), and would swing to the other extreme. Even madam-ing herself.

"Oh Cynthia!" she would gush as she opened the door, "Madam

wants tea. Could you give madam some tea, my girl?"

Mr. Koorn, who always wore a military cut, sides almost completely shorn, clean-shaven, had a schoolboyish look. Tall, trim, he would have looked younger than his wife had it not been for the thoughtful lines growing away from his saddened eyes. He was softly spoken, that is, on the rare occasion I heard his voice, in response, no doubt, to something Mrs. Koorn had said to him.

Both children were scrawny brats. The girl, like her mother, had masses of hair, although unlike the lady of the house who wore hers in a big bubble, the beehive, Lynnette sported a shiny ponytail that ended neatly in a gently pointed bush just at the waistline, an inch or so from the start of her seat.

The boy, Harad, seemed all ears, teeth, and knees.

Perhaps because of the contrast with children of my world, these two appeared to me exceedingly helpless and downright thoughtless. Not only did I cook for them, wash, clean, and pick up their litter; even their having a glass of milk and a biscuit was cause for my being summoned:

"Nanny, I want a glass of milk. I'd like a biscuit too, nanny."

Of course, later I would have to pick up the discarded plate and glass, empty or barely touched. But then, when their servant-filled life, at below bargain prices, assured them this "service with a smile," why would they have bothered learning skills they were never going to use?

The function of employment, for the African in my country, is to keep the African alive; that is, available as a worker. The usual rewards, not benefits, associated with employment — health, housing, education . . . a good life — come mostly with the pay envelope marked "whites only." Not surprising in a country that differentiated education so that Africans would never aspire to things not meant for them.

Since Aunt Dathini worked less than a ten-minute walk away from me, and since both her madam and mine worked Monday through to Friday, we spent a lot of time together. The houses where we worked were, certainly, no mansions. A couple of hours, that's all it took, and the morning's work was done.

I had to be in the house by early afternoon. That is when the two children returned from school. And as Mrs. Koorn had said when hiring me: "My girl, that is the one job I want you to make sure you do really nice." That is the one job where I know I never failed her. Not that I think she did not get much more than her money's worth, all told.

Little did I know what impact Aunt Dathini's coming to Cape Town would have on me. Daily she needled me: "But you, Sindiwe, shouldn't be scrubbing dirty white people's kitchens. For what did Bhuti educate you?" Her constant reminder that the dreariness she endured was something she could not accept for me, reminded me of my goals; goals that childbearing had obscured.

Thokozile was nearly three months old and still breast fed. The accommodation here was so bad the question of her coming to live with me just never cropped up. I tried to go home almost every night. That way, I could breast-feed her during the night and express and store two or even three feeds before I went to work — that is, on cool days, otherwise the milk spoilt, for we had neither electricity nor refrigeration. In the event, the short distance between Ottery and Guguletu was a blessing and I felt I wasn't doing too badly. Aunt Dathini would often accompany me on these nocturnal trips home, for she was fond of both my parents and they returned the sentiment. Many a time, we set out for Guguletu on foot and returned, hours later, by bus. Walking saved us both the fare and the long wait for buses, for neither Guguletu nor Ottery was well served in this respect.

Some nights, the two of us would end up together in her or my room. My Aunt Dathini would talk well into the night, about the stories of her life yesterday, her life on that very same day, or her life long, long ago. I have heard them all. And through them, she taught me, more than any other had, so much about life and living.

Hers had not been a life of planning. She had simply lived it as she saw safe. And lived it with gusto, denying herself little, not even that denied her by law: proof of which was even her being in Cape Town, without a pass.

Aunt Dathini loved to talk; she enjoyed conversation the way some people pursue a sport. She also liked herself not a little. So perhaps it is not surprising that her favorite subject was herself. Let me add, however, that her motives though, were not selfish. Simply, Dathini was an Entertainer.

146

The only regrets I ever heard come from her mouth were about her lack of education and lack of a pass that qualified her for employment in the urban areas of South Africa. As an "illegal," she, and all like her, were exploited mercilessly by the white women they worked for. All domestic workers are exploited. But those with no passes suffer even worse abuse. One of the few rules by which Aunt Dathini lived was that work under any conditions is far better than no work. Beneath those maid's overalls, however, beat the heart of a fighter.

As a young woman, she had been flogged, repeatedly, at home and at school, as she told me one night:

"I left school early. Very early. In those days we started school late. And then we stayed home as the seasons of the year determined. For planting and for harvest, we were home. I already had breasts, a big girl, and I was still in Standard One. Some of my age mates were being taken as wives, especially those who had not gone to school at all."

"*Iintombi zasesikolweni azendi*" ("Girls of school are not made wives") was common talk in the village. My aunt had had no intentions of, as she put it, "growing gray hair in my mother's house." She had stubbornly refused to go to school.

"The red youth had weekend parties, dances, and sing-songs (*imitshotsho*). I wanted to go, but my parents would not allow it.

"School and church went hand in hand. The families who sent their children to school also attended church. The ministers and the missionaries taught our parents that it was wrong for girls and boys or young women and young men to be together overnight. Our dances were evil, they said. But I wanted to go to the dances. I enjoyed singing. And, my child, could I sing?

"If I was forced to miss a dance, I would get complaints:

"'Dathini,' my age mates would say, 'the dance this past weekend was cold. We heard your voice was not among those singing for us.' When I sang, the ground threatened to crack open. I, Brother's child, had a voice."

On another night, angry at something her white woman had said or done, Aunt Dathini would lash out, "These white women bitches! This one doesn't know me. One day I'll fold her to a bundle not even her husband will be able to pick up. I swear, they'll need an ambulance to carry her the day I lay my hands on her."

One afternoon during our rest, she came in with wide, white-teeth smile, her whole face lit up.

"*Kanene, Sindiwe, yinton'itrongo ngesiNgesi?*" ("By the way, Sindiwe, what is jail in English?") "*Yijail,*" I told her ("It's jail").

"Yes," she remarked, "How could I forget? Who cares? *Uvile khon'ukuv'oku.*" ("Hearing, she did hear.")

Out came the story. My Aunt Dathini had had a fight with her *mlungu* woman. The latter had been left in no doubt as to the relationship existing, at least in Dathini's own mind, between the two of them. She, not Dathini, was the beggar:

"I never come and knock on your door and say I want work, medem. You see me in the bus stop and you want me," the medem had been told by an irate Dathini.

Hey, if that's not telling it like it is, what is?

That little exchange ended with Anti squeezing a rise from her employer who had been told: "I'm not in *trongweni.*" *Tronk*, the Afrikaans for jail, she must have recognized; Xhosa locative suffix and all.

Looking at her animated face, I thought, if she'd won the July Handicap, she could not have been more pleased with herself.

The indifferent transport system serving the African townships, terrible on any day of the week, is worse on Sunday. We had been waiting at the bus stop for over half an hour. There was nothing particularly noteworthy about that event. I had found an elderly lady already waiting. By and by, other would-be passengers had arrived and, by the time we made a bus sighting, there were about a dozen or so people waiting at the bus stop. The bus came and, jostling and pushing, everyone got in. I asked the elderly lady to go in before me but she declined. Puzzled, I stepped onto the bus. She had had to stand aside. She was going to work at getting onto the bus: "*Wag*, driver, *my kind!*" she pleaded. ("Wait, driver, my child.")

Left hand holding onto the bar at the door, right hand puts bag on second step of bus. Both hands reach and lift right leg and deposit same on first step of bus. Left leg catches up on own accord. Repeat.

Repeat once more. Finally, lady is in the bus; all the seats are taken by this time, of course!

All through the journey, from the last stop in Guguletu to the terminus in Claremont, I kept seeing the nightmare of a sixty-nine-year-old me lifting my leg with my hands to get onto a bus to go and be on my knees scrubbing, scrubbing, scrubbing . . . till WHEN? Till WHAT happened?

My mind recoiled from the horrendous eventuality.

If I had had any notion of making domestic work a lifetime career, the old lady I have just described cured me of that. I did not know how or when, but I was as sure as sure can be that I would get out! And get out while my two God-given knees could still hinge unaided.

My prayers were to be answered, much sooner than I thought and in ways I would not have imagined.

By the time Thokozile was a year old I was three months pregnant. Twenty-three years old.

Books on developmental psychology are silent about what must, surely, be the Womb Trap Stage of development. I refuse to believe I am a freak and I am too humble to think I could be that rarity, the exception which proves the rule.

Although birth control was beginning to be very accessible to African women in South Africa, it came heralded by a great many myths and shrouded in political controversy. It is unfortunate that the government favors birth control for us. That has been the kiss of death for birth control. We have become so conditioned by what the government has done to us that anything it says is good for us, we know has to be very bad for us.

Consider this, at the same time that blacks were being encouraged, vigorously, to participate in family-planning programs, whites were being encouraged in the opposite direction. This same government, urging us to have fewer children, was offering white families bonuses for having more than four.

Also, one of the reasons behind family-planning, supposedly, is that fewer children translate to a higher standard of living. Show me the childless African couple, professional couple, who have succeeded to a house in Bishopscourt. I know, personally, many a childless woman who, upon reaching old age, has suffered hunger pangs and worse, for her inadequate and color-differentiated government pension is not supplemented by occasional gifts of money from working offspring.

And remember, at the same time that the government was encouraging us to curb our wombs, our black wombs, the same government stepped up its immigration recruitment drive. The people who were being lured here had to have one criterion, and one only. They had to be white.

Clearly, the message was, fewer children will mean more to spread around. Except, the fewer applied to blacks only. And the spreading would be around whites only, home-grown and imported. Black politicians did not hesitate to point out such thinly disguised attempts at culling our numbers: "Genocide! Annihilation of Africans!" they screamed.

It must be obvious by now that I did not plan any of my three children. However, as with each birth I weakened, financially, that is, this third pregnancy was the hardest on me. Even with a loving husband, a well-paid loving husband, three children one on top of the other would have been a strain on our budget. We had no budget. And soon, we had no we either.

Forced to grow

"**C**ynthia, I am sorry I have to let you go. Why didn't you tell me you are pregnant? Your husband told me. He also said he doesn't want you working hard now because you have very difficult deliveries."

"But, Medem, I am only four months . . . I want to . . ."

"NO, NO. And, NO. I can't keep you here if your husband doesn't want you working. You know the law! I'm very sorry, my girl."

My husband! Only the previous Wednesday, June 26, 1966, little suspecting I would not set eyes on him for nearly two decades, I had helped my husband pack. I had made his provisions and gone to Cape Town station to see him onto the train, and waited on the platform till it pulled out; and waved my goodbyes. The next four months were to be a nightmare!

Four days later, June having thirty days, it was the end of the month. I received two things from Mrs. Koorn, my employer: the first, the eagerly awaited thirty rand, my monthly wage for the cleaning, cooking, and nannying.

The second, this thunderbolt: I was no longer in her employ!

Unbeknown to me, before my dearest's departure he had done me one last favor, a favor Mrs. Koorn was painstakingly explaining to me.

She had had four days to adjust to my leaving. No wrench to her in any event. A pair of hands was all I represented. There were thousands more where this pair came from. My world did a mad topsy-turvy turn. Wordlessly, I turned and walked out of the house, crossed the small backyard and entered "my room," the garage I shared with the family car.

It was true I had to deliver by Caesarean section, thanks to a contracted pelvis. Of course, it was also true I was pregnant. However, I was strong. I hadn't started showing. I hardly show till the end of the seventh month. And then, slightly. I had counted on working for at least three or four months more.

Blindly, I paced the concrete floor. My mind became objective to the point of disembodiment, a thing apart.

The tears boiling inside me would not spill out of the dry eyes. No sound would the aching throat let out. I had lost all control of my body. No part of what had been, until then, my body would obey the mind that refused to give the orders I, somewhere deep inside me, wanted carried out. Only the feet moved. And then, not according to my will. Why else would they go on moving when I was wearied and wanted to lie down and think? And then when I wanted my feet to move usefully so I could pack, they became lead. Think! Of course I was thinking. That was what I had been doing all along. Not knowing I was.

Only, the thoughts were one thought, or a chain of thoughts. Or were they the answer?

WHAT WILL WE EAT? RENT? . . . RENT, WHAT WILL WE EAT? EAT? RENT? And on and on and on. The mind echoed the refrain.

I do not know how long I had been in there looking at my mind when one of the Koorn children came to tell me the family would be going out that evening and would give me a lift to the bus terminus if I were ready by six o'clock.

I was not that distraught that I was blind to this kind gesture. If anything, grief had sharpened my wits. The ride would save me the more arduous leg of the journey; the half-an-hour walk to the train station. It would also save me about fifteen cents; the cost of the third-class single-journey train ticket. Also, I had a suitcase, packed to carry. And, I was, after all, pregnant.

I was ready long before the set hour, not unaware of the need the Koorns would feel of assuring themselves that I had truly vacated their premises. Many are the tales of servants who had succeeded in carrying entire households away, notwithstanding their lack of any means of transportation.

I was driven to Claremont Station, more convenient for getting buses to the townships. All the way to the bus terminus Mrs. Koorn prattled incessantly about my husband's concern. I could almost hear the syrupy solicitude in his voice by the time the car dropped me off, marking my farewell to the Koorns!

Thus rescued from the deadening drudgery of domestic work, I was plunged straight into the gaping hell of dire poverty.

Even then my anxiety and anger had been based on misinformation: Yes, I was unemployed and I was pregnant. But I did not have a husband. I had been banking on even one such as mine — ill-paid and tight-fisted. I had thought he would soon be back, and that my financial hardship would stem from my not being able to count on the thirty rand I could call my own, come month-end. Whilst in service, I hadn't had to worry about my own meals. Now I had to feed myself and the two infant children, my daughters. I soon learnt I was worse off than I realized.

At age twenty-three, married, mother of nearly three children, I was sans husband. Not divorced. No. My husband became my former husband through a much more simple method than divorce; the method commonly referred to as "he is dead wearing a hat" ("*ufe ethwele umnqwazi*"). This saying, I think, comes from the custom of Xhosa men having to wear a hat once they have gone through circumcision and been, therefore, proclaimed MEN. Dead implies no longer there, of no use to us, or, simply, ineffectual. "Dead wearing a hat" means, therefore, the husband no longer performs those duties usually associated with that role — functions such as those of provider, protector, lover, and father. He is dead in the role of family head. However, as he is "wearing a hat," he is walking around physically appearing alive.

153

My husband achieved this status by the simple action of going on a three-week visit to his parents. A visit that has lasted to date. When next heard of, he was in Johannesburg! Johannesburg is about a thousand miles north of Cape Town, where we lived. And his parents live in Matatiele, in the Transkei, some five hundred miles from Cape Town in an easterly direction! To be fair, though, I assumed the three weeks period. He never actually said three weeks. But I may be pardoned for making the mistake. What unloving wife wouldn't do the same when her about-to-stop-loving husband casually mentions one evening, "I am leaving to go and see my parents. Expect me on the sixteenth of July."

Not backward in my arithmetic, I calculated three weeks from the 26th of June. The year was 1966!

How I have regretted not making quite certain we were talking, or rather thinking, of the same year. For all I knew, my husband could casually have strolled back any year on the sixteenth day of July. And who could blame him for the little misunderstanding?

"How silly of you, darling, not to have realized I hadn't meant 16th July 1966, the same year I was leaving, but 16th July 1986!"

Late in July, I received a letter with no return address from my husband. From the postmark I could not tell where it had been mailed. How long is he going to be away? I worried. He was in Johannesburg, he said, adding he would soon be on his way to his parents.

As there was no address, all I could do was wait. I waited.

Soon, another letter came. This time he had included an address. This was his brother's address, he stated. I hadn't known he had a brother in Johannesburg. But, knowing our extended family system, this piece of news surprised me but little. Besides, I had better and more pressing concerns. It was past what I had thought would be his date of return. He still had not favored me with any information about that. My alarm grew.

I replied expressing fury at the liberty he had taken in giving up my job for me. In no uncertain terms, I reminded him of the pregnancy he seemed to have remembered only long enough to terminate my employment. "I should be attending (prenatal) clinic. The baby's layette ought to be making an appearance via the simple well-known process of buying," I explained, adding, "that means money, which, as I'm no longer working, means YOU give it to me."

The cat took to the hearth, as amaXhosa, my people, say when real no-nonsense shame-aside destitution hits a home. Cats are to hearths what speculators must be to gold-diggings. However, when the cat occupies the hearth on a permanent basis, this indicates the hearth has been out of use for a far longer period than usually is the case.

Cats, unlike speculators, believe the adage, "too much of a good thing is bad." They are after warmth, not roasting themselves. As we have no other means of cooking except the three-legged iron pot over the open fire burning bright underneath, no fire is no food. In our house, the proverbial cat was about to build a mansion on the hearth!

Father was away at sea on one of the deep-sea fishing trawlers that are an integral part of Cape Town's famous fishing industry. Having recently lost his job at the garage where he had worked as long as I had known him, too old to be readily employable, this had been the only job he had been able to land: galley-boy. Mother had gone to the village we had left many, many years ago to come to Cape Town, to be by the death-bed of her father. I was in charge. Five younger siblings, ranging in age from five to thirteen, depended on me for their very existence! And then there were my two children.

By early August we had run out of every conceivable necessity: money, mealie-meal, mealie-rice, bread, flour, candles, kerosene, matches, soap, Vaseline. You name it, we didn't have it. And there was nowhere and no one to turn to, except me.

On a sluggish grayish day in August, the month of my birth, I found myself on the bridge on the Klipfontein road overlooking the railway line in Guguletu. I had left the house very early, before any of the children were up. I had also left without the breakfast we couldn't have. There was nothing in the house. Not one grain of corn!

As I stood there looking down onto the tracks my short adulthood flitted by rapidly in my mind's eye. Stupid. Hasty. Profoundly fertile. I had rushed into a marriage my parents disapproved of at age nineteen. Four years later, I was within weeks of having my third child. My husband had left. I had no job. I had no money. I had no food. I had no rent. I had no hope.

How long I stood there dully contemplating jumping at the sight of an approaching train, I don't know. It was getting dark when I entered St. Mary Magdalene, the Anglican church roughly halfway between the bridge and my home.

"The doors of a church are never locked," father had once said, ". . . because whenever anyone should need a haven, physical or spiritual, God's house should be there, waiting and available."

In that church, that evening, I cried; and I prayed. Both activities were no strangers to me. I have, since then, known both, together, and separately. There, I received strength from God. But not money. Not food. By the time I returned home, it was well past suppertime.

I went to the butcher and asked for credit. Not so we could eat. Would I be that frivolous? I asked for and was given, five sheep heads. The cost to me would be one rand or a hundred cents. The idea was to clean and cook these and then sell them. At forty cents each, selling price, I would be making 100% profit. The only outlay would be my hands and my strength, lots of the latter — transforming a hairy, bloody, matty head of a sheep to a smooth, clean, cooked, and enticing item of food is not for the weak of body. I felt better. I was in business.

Five days a week I took five sheep heads from the butcher, always paying him the next day, after sales. I perfected, to an art, the method of preparing and cooking this delicacy:

1. Rinse sheep head in cold water, thoroughly, until there is no trace of blood on wool.
2. Let most of the water run off by pressing hands in downward motion from mouth area towards base or severed end.
3. Put head in airy, sunny place for at least half an hour to allow wool to dry. Outside is best for this, but beware of dogs. Dogs have an underdeveloped sense of social responsibility and proprietorship.
4. Make a log fire.
5. Place head on flame, less than five minutes each time, to singe wool.
6. Remove and using old table knife and plucking, scraping movements, remove burnt wool.
7. Repeat 5 and 6, exposing different areas to flame until only stub-

156

ble remains.

8. Using red-hot flat-iron rods and ironing movements, go over stubble until surface is smooth to touch; use cylindrical rods for all apertures.
9. Immerse in almost boiling water and, using pot-scraper, scrub clean.

For those customers who want to cook the head themselves, this is all the preparation necessary. However, most customers preferred not to be bothered by the cumbersome work involved. The next stage then is:

1. Take a very sharp knife and describe a line down the center of the head, from crown, down the bridge, to the lower lip.
2. Using a sharp ax and following this line, split the head open.
3. Rinse the inside thoroughly, washing out the sticky liquid under the tongue, through the nasal cavity, etc.
4. Put in pot with enough water to cover, add salt and bring to boil.
5. Simmer till tender (two to three hours).
6. Cool.

Another of my husband's rambling letters came. In this one he surprised even me, and I had thought I knew the extent of his feebleness of reason. He wanted me to join him in Johannesburg where, he stated, he was now working. This was a suggestion bordering on insanity! Africans in South Africa did not just move from one town to another at the drop of a hat, or because they so wished. My husband was asking me to break the law. Moreover, by leaving the area of the Western Cape where I had permission to live and work, I would be risking losing that permission, to say nothing of the jail sentence I faced if found in Johannesburg where I had no business to be without permission. Permission to reside or work in one urban area was not only not transferable, it excluded the right to be in another. If he was willing to be an illegal worker in Johannesburg, that was his privilege. But he was not dragging me into that kind of mess. I was in enough already. Since his departure, I had had no support of any kind from my husband.

Of course, it would be this time around that I would balloon by the fifth month. As I grew with each passing day, I began to have a serious problem. Not a dress to wear. Not for dressing up, nothing fancy. The question was how to cover my body.

Aunt Dathini came to the rescue. Several sizes bigger than I will ever be, she gave me one of her own dresses. And, God knows, she had few herself.

This was one of those two-seams-only affairs; just the side seams running through from sleeve to hem. This dress had three-quarter sleeves not unlike the legs of bell-bottom pants. Dark green in color, it was liberally splashed with vaguely formed flowers. Black. It was not a bad dress, I suppose. But, of course, even a big dress has a hard time substituting for a maternity dress.

I looked like Humpty-Dumpty in a sack. At least, that is how I felt I looked. Thoroughly ridiculous. But that beat being naked, in my book.

To this day, I will not wear that combination of colors. I absolutely, unreservedly, and irreconcilably loathe black on a dark-green background.

A few letters had come and gone between Luthando and me when I realized that although we were exchanging letters we were not carrying on a correspondence. I would receive a letter from him and, several days later, send off mine to him. In my letter I might allude to some of the questions or pronouncements he had raised, I don't know. However, I do know that I never received, in his, any answers to my questions nor word of assurance to quell my growing anxiety.

"I need to buy napkins for the baby. I need money for fare to the clinic. I need food for the children. There is no rent money. What do you think we eat, stones?"

"Thank you for your solicitude, I am now in line for a cave. We have received notice of eviction. Where is the money you said you were sending?"

To such letters, explicit, no nonsense, direct, and demanding answers, my husband would "reply" telling me everything except what I was most anxious to hear, which was news of the amount he was sending and the date on which I might expect it. I would send back a screeching, ranting letter in which I had left out only those swear words I didn't know. I would, in due course, get an infuriatingly calm reply telling me about the cattle in his parents' home, that threatened to destroy the kraal they were enclosed in, because of sheer numbers! The implication being that I chose to starve as I could

158

always go to his father's house and be fed.

This I could not do without letting my parents down yet again. Luthando had not complied with the lobola negotiations. If I went to his father's home, served the apprenticeship (*ukuhota*) that all new wives (*oomakoti*) have to serve — that would have implied no more money was owing; would have left my parents in a weakened position for making any claim — certainly no more lobola would have come to them.

Then, one day, my patience was rewarded. What I wanted most to hear was there for me to read —

". . . enough for you and the children for about a month. I sent the money to TEBA to make sure it does not go astray. Let me know you have received it, as soon as you do."

No pardoned sinner ever felt a greater sense of redemption! The Transvaal Employment Bureau for Africans (TEBA) had offices in Langa, in the Western Cape. This called for a fare of about twenty cents. Having borrowed the fare, I was at these offices, bright and early. I planned to proceed from there to the city to make the almost late purchases for the baby's layette.

"There is no money here for that name," jabbed the cold, clipped, clearly correct voice of the gentleman on the other side of the counter.

Surely, he was mistaken?

"Maybe he sent it in my maiden name," I blurted, coming up for air.

Incredulity on his white brow which had ascended a clear half of an inch chasing the hairline.

"And what, pray, is YOUR maiden name, my dear?"

"Cynthia Magona," croaked a voice I didn't recognize. And, in numbing anticipation, knowing and refusing to accept the horror, "He may have used my clan name, MamTolo."

Was it pity, scorn, or naked triumph? With the slightest soupçon of sarcasm in his voice, bushy eyebrows were now in real danger of getting wedded to receding hairline, forever setting the august gentleman's face in a mold of haughty studied indifference —

"You people waste our time. Every day, the same thing. Day in, day out. Over and over. Again and again." Mimicking a black woman's voice: "My husband says there is money here for me. My money is here from my boyfriend." Returning to his audience, "Well Mrs. whatever or Miss whatever . . . at this office, there is no money for you. Now please stop wasting my time." Frosty metallic blue eyes said, "*Voetsek!*" ("Get out, buzz off, be gone!")

Thank God the beast was such a thoroughbred! The slightest show of kindness would have been more than enough encouragement for me to disintegrate, lose myself, and open the floodgates. No such relief was open to me. I had urgent business to attend to. The bus-fare to Langa had been a loan. How was I to get back to Guguletu?

I remembered a very distant relative who lived in Langa. Matshangisa was a childhood friend of mother's and had, moreover, married one of father's second cousins. I had to ask for directions to her house, for I do not believe I had ever set foot there before that day. Fortunately, I remembered her daughter's name and the fact that the house was near a certain school. Children's names are more important in the African townships than those of their parents. The children are better known because most adults are addressed by their children's names — so-and-so's mother, so-and-so's father. It is the height of rudeness to call a grown person by name. Also, children are the real inhabitants of the townships. Most adults are away a good part of the day. They are the smiling, uniformed servants of white homes and white businesses; coming home only long enough to replenish their spent bodies so that they may resume their chores the next day, and the next, smiling.

As luck would have it, Matshangisa was home, off duty from her hospital-maid's job. The ancestors were with me that day. I rested. I was offered a meal. And Matshangisa gave me a whole rand, five times more than I had asked for. She also gave me some foodstuffs to take home and sent me away feeling a lot more whole than I had felt when I arrived at her home. The many faces of healing! The many faces of prayer!

That is the day I divorced my husband. In my heart. Writing to him would cost me half a cent for the envelope, four cents for the stamp, another half a cent for the paper. That was half a loaf of brown bread, the cheapest bread, and a box of matches or a quarter bottle of kerosene. That, I reasoned on the bus ride home, was a waste of time and money.

160

TO MY CHILDREN'S CHILDREN

Although I did not know it then, by the time I reached home I had joined the invisible league of women, worldwide — the bearers and nurturers of the human race whom no government or institution recognizes or rewards, and no statistician captures and classifies.

Backbreaking scrubbing of sheep heads. Fetch them from the butcher's carrying the heavy box on your head. Wash and dry them. Over the fire they go. Scrape. Clean. Cook. Five days a week. Monday through to Thursday. And again on Saturday. Friday was clinic day. Five times five sheep heads. At forty cents each, selling price was ten rand. Five was clear profit, the other half belonged to the butcher.

One rand was the train-fare to and from Cape Town and maybe an orange or perhaps, a banana, fish and chips, or meat. Offal, that is. Somerset Hospital, where I had to attend clinic, is about ten minutes, by bus, from the center of town. I had to walk there and back; not for the exercise either. Another rand was used each week to buy a napkin or a vest or a nightie in preparation for the new arrival. Two rands had to be put aside for the R8,05 monthly rent. That left a rand for food and anything else. We did without anything else. And, for food, we used mealie-meal in different textures and guises. As porridge in the morning, with sugar (we dispensed with milk, and there were times even the sugar was hard to come by). Mealie-meal for dinner, with gravy from the sheep heads we could not afford to eat unless they threatened spoiling. The sheep brains were a constant in our diet.

This foraging, above all, earned me the precious prize of a layette of half a dozen napkins, two vests, and two nighties; a receiving blanket and a ninety-nine cents shawl (to hide the shame of the absence of a blanket). Everything, the cheapest available!

On the last Friday in October I went to the Somerset Hospital for the regular weekly clinic. During the examination the doctor began asking questions that sent a shiver down my leaden spine.

"No," I thought, "God would not do that to me." The words of the doctor, however, poured cold water on naked ballooned me, lying there on the examination table. And my shaky faith in my God, seeing as to how He had let so much happen to me already, did not much comfort me.

"I think you are having twins," the doctor said, little realizing I might have nothing, having died, instantaneously of a heart attack, at his innocent words. What did he know of the fearful pain his words inflicted? Was he aware of the half-a-dozen napkins in my layette? Did he know of the father who was "dead wearing a hat"? I doubt he even saw the hot tears streaming down my shivering face. He, all professional, had turned away to allow me the luxury of getting dressed with dignity into my borrowed overall.

Bright sunlight surprised me as I crossed the courtyard from one wing of the hospital to another. I was going to X-rays and confirmation of the doctor's suspicions. Many years ago when I had been young and stupid, even then certain of my productivity, I had actually prayed that God would bless me with, believe it or not, twins. Three sets of twins: girls, girls, boys. Was my idiotic prayer about to be answered?

My shattered belief in man swiftly generalized itself to include HIM. But, incongruously, I was still, even at that moment of collapsed faith, sending a silent but most heartfelt and urgent prayer: "Please, dear God, don't let it be twins."

The predicament twins would put me in! Divide the sinfully skimpy layette I had for one baby by two. I'm not sure I would not have killed myself.

Luckily, the X-rays showed it was a false alarm. The baby was a breach presentation, which threatened to split open the twice-opened and thus weakened scar of my tummy. The verdict: the baby would be taken out the next day.

The hospital wanted to send me, by ambulance, to Groote Schuur Hospital where, for some reason, I was being transferred. I had left home that morning thinking I had three weeks to make arrangements. So, I pleaded with the doctor to allow me to go home first. I promised to go to Groote Schuur that same day, before nightfall.

It is at times like these that the hardship of living without telephones becomes a curse. I found someone to come and stay with the children. Left whatever food money I had. Sent word to Aunt Dathini about the turn of events. Alerted Nolusapho's Aunt Dina, down the road, to keep an eye on things. Sent a telegram to my husband; and left for the hospital.

I arrived there just before supper. But that did not help me get any. I was admitted and put to bed with a "NIL PER MOUTH" sign hanging at the foot of my bed, warning all and sundry I was headed for the doctor's scalpel the next morning.

Sandile, my only son, was born four months, one week, and five days after his father's desertion: a bouncing eight pounds, eight ounces. Yes, he was three and a half weeks early. Thank God!

My husband must have gone to a florist as soon as he received the telegram I had sent him. The baby was not quite a day old when no less august a person than the matron herself came to visit me. She had calmed my husband, she told me, my husband who was so distraught at not being near me.

The matron was immensely impressed at the loving, caring, and concern she had sensed in him. Luthando had phoned the hospital, all the way from Johannesburg, and demanded to speak to the matron. And, although how he did this I do not know, an enormous vase, filled with the most exquisite flowers you can imagine, stood proudly on the night table next to my bed. So big and ornate was the arrangement, all the nurses, day and night shift, came to "ooh" and "aah" over it.

"Is your husband away on duty, Mama?" the matron asked, intrigued. I nodded my reply, too stunned to talk. She patted my bedspread — no doubt mistaking my inability to utter words to my fretting for my absent love — and made soothing tut-tut noises before leaving. A smile on her face. I was a little sorry to see her go without the conversation she had sought from me. I couldn't help it that she had come and so muddled my thoughts.

If ever there was a court case about Luthando's criminal neglect, he had made certain he had a witness of repute. And as if that were not enough cunning to be lodged in one body, he had actually made me an accomplice in his design. How well he knew me. How perceptive of him to know, with absolute certainty, I would as soon staple my tongue to the roof of my mouth as blurt out, "My husband has deserted me." Too proud, too stupid, too shy.

I blamed myself for the failure of our relationship. "Surely," I told myself, "only a flaw in me could have led me to choose such a man for a husband." I am not one who finds it easy to own up, never mind confess, and to strangers at that, that I am easy to dupe. Luthando knew that about me. Knew it before I knew it about myself. For that is what my inability to tell that matron that my husband had been bullshitting taught me that day.

The bed next to mine was occupied by a very large woman with skin as black as the isipingo berries that dye your mouth, tongue, teeth, and everything else, black for days. Her husband, who came faithfully every evening, was just as dark. He was also not a slim man.

Neither of these two people could read or write. They had put crosses instead of signatures on the forms consenting to the operation the day the wife was admitted. Since they understood no English I had interpreted, for the medical staff of this hospital (and most others) knew no Xhosa.

This woman and I had given birth to sons. For both of us our first. Her beaming husband made my empty visitor's chair look emptier, each night. But it was on our last day at Groote Schuur Hospital that I felt my husband's neglect most keenly. If Luthando had stabbed me with a butcher's knife, my heart would not have bled more than it did that day:

We were discharged just after breakfast. Less than an hour thereafter, this woman had left. Her husband had hired a taxi, had come with same to help her carry the baby, carry her bags, and help them to the car. He handled his wife as if she were the most fragile thing on this earth. They left for the single men's hostels where, with other migrant laborers, her husband stayed. His wife, no doubt, lived there too, while in Cape Town to visit her husband.

Remember how educated I felt I was. And there I was, waiting, not for my husband but for any one of my relatives who had taken pity on me and was, even then, on the way to take me home, by public transport, stitches and all.

I waited. Lunch came and since I was no longer a patient, I couldn't expect to be served a meal. I was not disappointed. When it began to look as if afternoon tea would find me still there, I picked up my baby, picked up my bag, said a feeble "goodbye" to my erstwhile roommates, and left. Not giving the flowers a second glance.

Groote Schuur Hospital, picturesque, stands on a hill. Each downhill step I took the tightly pulled, stitched, and clipped muscles of my midriff protested. My legs, after days of inactivity, felt like jelly. I tottered, the baby weighing twice as much as he really did. I walked down that hill not seeing where I was going. Tears were pouring down my face. I was so wretched that I was past caring who saw me cry.

When I got to the Main Road at the bottom of the hill, because it was Sunday I had a longish wait. That did nothing to help me calm down. When the bus to Claremont finally came, I got in and immediately had several offers of a seat. Downstairs. This was the time of segregated seating — whites sat downstairs and lucky we had the upstairs all to ourselves. There were exceptions though. And an unaccompanied, obviously distressed new mother qualified as one.

By the time I reached home my bout of self-pity had subsided. Reality has that effect.

I had undeniable business to attend to: three infants to raise, my own life to rebuild; and no tools.

The picture is clear today for it has not, for one day, left me. I had a pot boiling away on the primus stove. The children waited and waited. The pot boiled away on the stove. The children waited for the food to cook.

First, Thembeka, the eldest, always a sleepy child, dropped off. I scooped her up from the floor and put her to bed.

Sandile, the baby, was no problem. Mother's milk is always there.

One by one, the other children (my siblings) fell asleep. As I took occasional promising peeps at the pot, one by one, the children fell asleep.

Thokozile was the last to do so. I put her next to the others on the bed. I switched off the stove and gratefully crept into bed myself; silently sending a prayer of thanks to God for the gift of hope: without the hope that they would be getting something to eat, the children would have been restless, crying for food. They had fallen asleep unaware that nothing more than God's clean water was in that pot busily boiling way on the primus stove.

But, as an old saying goes, thunder passes ("*liduduma lidlule*"). Thunder, that harbinger of crop-destroying rains, of floods that sweep away the very soil and, not infrequently, of death by lightning, is held in awe and great fear by my people. It is therefore equated with all things ruinous to man. Yet the recognition is there that no one person is sole heir to all the trouble there can be all the time. And I knew that even my hardship would come to an end. So I had to live each day with tenacious hope that my life would change for the better.

But, I could not have done it alone. No one, however determined, could do that alone: credit from Mr. Njobe the butcher meant back-breaking work. It also spelled, very clearly, the difference between being alive and being dead. To go to the hospital, I had needed a dress. Every Thursday evening, for the last two and half months of my pregnancy, I had sent one of my sisters to Nomvuyo Ngcelwane who had just had a baby, to borrow her overall. Every Friday morning, I had donned this pink all-cotton garment with black lace collar and, respectable, had sallied forth to clinic. Came back, washed and returned the overall in the evening. Another woman, a neighbor and a friend, Mrs. Nokholeji Gobodo, used to send the "leftovers my spoilt brats won't eat." Some of these were suspiciously fresh look-ing! Then there was the milkman. I don't know how he kept his job. With the understanding he showed me when I couldn't pay the milk bill, he would never become a dairy owner. But his wealth is greater. Innocent of any training in psychology or psychiatry, he had the gift of healing broken spirits without appearing even to try. His smile. His kindly banter. My Carl Rogers!

My exceeding good fortune began to dawn on me. I was alive. I was healthy. I lived among people, themselves poor, wealthy in their knowledge that their own security lay in lending a hand.

My husband had left me young enough still to be optimistic: I believed I was equal to the task at hand. But above all, I came to see I was not just alone; I was free. Free of him. Free to be.

So many women's lives are hindered, hampered, and ruined by husbands who will not leave long after they have ceased to be hus-bands or fathers to their families. Dead wearing a hat, these men actively and energetically visit untold woe on those they once had loved. I was not thus afflicted, I saw.

It is strange that it should have been the loss of Luthando, the husband I no longer loved, the one person in my life who meant the

166